There's a Spy in my Soup

Elizabeth Blake

First published by Dog Ear Publishing
4010 W. 86th Street, Ste H
Indianapolis, IN 46268
www.dogearpublishing.net

ISBN: 978-145750-035-0

This book is printed on acid-free paper.

Printed in the United States of America

Remembering Tom,
with love

CONTENTS

NOTE:

As this is a story related to the CIA, some details have been blurred, changed and added because of security concerns. The names and locations of two actual overseas CIA stations are fictionalized to prevent their positive identification.

The story is not intended to spill CIA secrets nor to portray the Agency in any negative light. It is merely the story of a family who moved around the world, and the experiences encountered during that adventure, all while living as a CIA family overseas. Acknowledging various hardships, the entire family nevertheless agrees that the opportunities we encountered far outweighed the temporary disadvantages.

The CIA has reviewed this book and, having withdrawn its original objections after nearly two years of dispute, does not now pose any security objection to its publication.

A Kaleidoscope of Memories

O ur trip lasted almost twenty-seven years. In that time, we boiled enough drinking water to float a ship. We killed scorpions and tarantulas— and watched lizards run free— in our homes. We filled our upright freezer with trout so large that they stretched the entire width of the unit. Food was delivered surreptitiously to our home by black market trucks in the dark of night. We tromped through steamy tropical forests to gaze in wonder at the ruins and relics of lost civilizations. We loaded hundreds of rolls in film in our cameras. And we ate some *very* strange meals.

We developed interests in hand blown glass, pre-Columbian artifacts, Greek and Roman art and archaeology, World War II European battle sites, Latin American history and watercolor paintings by a Belgian artist who became our friend.

We treasure our friendships with people we met along the way. Some endured being on planes hijacked by terrorists. Others lost all their belongings when evacuated from posts suddenly overcome by danger and violence. A few came under fire and were taken hostage, and, sadly enough, some were killed while in the service of our country.

Using different languages sometimes led to funny moments. Once, while shopping, I confidently asked for "a dozen Thursdays" and another time, wanting boneless chicken, requested "chicken without eggs." So, we laughed with understanding when a friend, taking slacks with a broken zipper to a tailor, asked if they could put new lightning in her husband's pants.

It was pointed out to us that in the northern hemisphere pigs' tails, like water going down a drain, curl in a counter-clockwise direction, while in the southern hemisphere they spiral clockwise. Challenged to find out what happens right on the equator, we headed out to settle the burning question and found that there they hang straight down.

We always were grateful to be able to travel and see and do. We visited fairy tale castles. We were sobered by some of the sites remaining from the days of Nazi inhumanities. And we were charmed by quaint and colorful villages scattered here and there on the hillsides of a dozen different countries.

We think of our life in terms of a series of mental snapshots. Dan's parents, when trying to date a memory of person or event, always used cars as their reference point. For us, though, it's a simple matter to attach time and place to our memories. We don't have to think about it, really. We lived in easy to define blocks of time and a certain flavor belongs to each of our overseas posts. The different tours reflect vividly specific colors and textures, people and events.

In a way, ours was an episodic existence, often lacking the generally seamless transition of one day to the next or one year to another, which both Dan and I experienced during our childhoods. Even so, because it was the life we were living together, it came to seem perfectly normal.

As we roamed the world for the CIA, our life was full of flashes of intense times that were funny and sad, stressful and invigorating, light and dark. One memory triggers another, set in a different time and place. But the things we remember are related nonetheless, because they meld in a kaleidoscope of mental snapshots, a kaleidoscope of memories.

Spooks in Pinstripe Suits

Less flashy than that fellow Bond, James Bond, Dan is nevertheless my favorite "spy." It's true that he prefers hamburgers to caviar, just as he wears a watch that doesn't send messages, doesn't take pictures, doesn't track missiles. It just tells time. He never piloted his own mini-submarine in a chase through Caribbean waters or dangled from a helicopter, tossing bombs at the bad guys.

He's just a guy who happened to spend an entire career with the CIA. Sure and steady, decent and honest, quiet and funny and down-to-earth real, he's tall and slender, a nice looking man with a cleft in his chin, who usually can be found wearing crisp chinos and a button-down plaid shirt. He tells corny jokes, makes beautiful pieces of furniture in his basement workshop, is nuts about fishing and loves coconut cream pie.

He is secure enough in himself to just be who he is, with no need to be the life of the party. Dan is not one to try to impose his beliefs and views on others, although if the kids announced their intention to take up cross-country skiing, for example, he might suggest that they pick a *small* country. He has always believed that money is less important than ideals, and being happy at what one does is the real key to fulfillment.

Any blemishes on this guy? Well, there is this thing about sometimes being clumsy. It's a yearly ritual at our house for him to get out the hedge trimmer and, on the second or third swipe through the greenery, proceed to cut the electrical cord in half. He almost never works in the yard without drawing blood, and I make it a point to stay home, close to the phone and 911 when he has plans to use his electric saw.

As for me, I'm Liz, a happy person with dark brown hair, now tending toward gray, and clear blue eyes, someone with a love of flying kites in the sunshine. And at this point we're definitely closing in fast on becoming senior citizens, something that fills me with stunned disbelief. Basically I'm happiest being a homebody, although it always was a delight to return to work at our local weekly newspaper each time we rotated back to Virginia from overseas. I'm amused by puzzles of all kinds yet nearly flunked geometry in high school. I think being rich is feeling snug and comfortable and full of contentment so, despite what those bank statements stuffed in the desk drawer indicate, I am very rich, indeed.

Together Dan and I are a team, lucky enough to have found something to laugh about virtually every day of our married life. We figure it's a bonus for us that his quiet strength is a counterpart to my own high spirits.

We have three kids. The oldest is actually named William, but during his toddler days we noted a resemblance to the jolly man pictured on the box of oatmeal in our pantry and, as such things go, "Penn" just stuck, somehow. Lucky for Sam that we weren't committed to nicknames for each of our offspring. When he was a newborn he looked a lot like Mr. Magoo. Completing our family is McKinley. We gave her no middle name, so for years her grandmother offered suggestions, like she was some sort of fill-in-the-blank contest.

When we started our odyssey, we carried along our first-born child who was not yet one month old, and each of us was equally clueless about the scope of the adventure ahead of us.

Later, Sam became the very first American diplomatic baby born in one South American country, in a clinic where the doctor used a piece of resonating wood shaped like a miniature baseball bat instead of a stethoscope, and the water for the sparking new pink bathtub in the "luxury suite" was carried upstairs in buckets.

By the time Kinley joined us, born in an Andean missionary hospital built on the sloping shoulders of an extinct volcano, protesters in the "great tuna boat conflict" were surrounding the embassy compound and pelting it with over-ripe bananas.

Dan was always curious about the world and since working for the Central Intelligence Agency sounded incredibly fascinating and funky, he leaped at the chance to join up with the "spooks." He hoped his job would take him to faraway places, never daring to believe that ultimately he would be sent out eight different times.

Whenever he was sent on assignment to a foreign country, the kids and I went with him, naturally, like professional camp followers. Each time we packed up for another move, Dan's enthusiasm buoyed us, filling us with excitement about what lay ahead in the next place we would call home.

Little kids grew up to be big kids, thinking that all of it— the moving, the different languages, the jungles, the oceans, the ancient ruins, the King's palace just down the street and around the corner— was routine. They felt sorry for friends who never got to move. They looked at us, startled, with little round eyes and little round mouths and asked, "What happened?" when we mentioned that Gramma and Grandad lived in the same house for forty years.

We're aware that sometimes CIA people are visualized as being part of an evil empire, trench-coated characters with hats pulled low on heads, clutching magnifying glasses. Our reaction to the perception that we are wicked, slithery creatures? Yes. Yes, we are. We joke about it from time to time. Maybe there's a bit of perverse pride in being so regarded, particularly when we know just how normal we are. And we think what wonderful luck it was that Dan worked for the CIA and dragged us along.

So how did it all begin?

It was in the mid-sixties and Dan was finishing his last semester of college. Eight years had passed since he began his undergraduate studies, not because he was slow but because a four-year stint as a survival instructor in the Air Force interrupted the educational process. At last he had settled on what he wanted to do with his life. A much-admired family friend had served with the Office of Strategic Services during World War II and stories about her exotic and fascinating service, as well as his own military travel and a natural interest in world affairs, combined to fuel a passionate hope that he would qualify for a position with the Central Intelligence Agency.

So he spent his final Thanksgiving vacation from school filling out pages and pages of the Agency's job application. He sent it in, then waited for more than a month before getting a phone call one day. Someone on the other end of the line requested that he present himself at an office in suburban Maryland the following week. He was scheduled to take an exam, covering such fields as history, English and foreign affairs, sort of like an advanced version of the Scholastic Aptitude Test college hopefuls take today.

After taking the test, he waited again. This time it dragged on for three months. His background investigation was being conducted and security officers were interviewing friends, neighbors and classmates. They talked to coworkers, professors and former employers. They were looking for anything that might prove him to be a security risk or show that he was an otherwise unsuitable candidate for employment.

At the time I was teaching second grade in Dan's hometown and we were engaged to be married the following summer. So CIA conducted a background check on me, too.

Actually, some aspects of our engagement were hardly the stuff dreams are made of. Not everyone joined wholeheartedly in our dance of joy. Namely, our mothers. The two were about as different as it is possible to be. Dan's mother was portly, proper and educated. Both contentious and funny, she was a minor grande dame, prideful of her place in the hierarchy of small town, old town, Maryland. Though from a modest childhood background that inferred no right to be imperious and domineering, she tended to bear down upon others like a battleship, with all guns blazing.

My mother, on the other hand, was slender and breezily elegant, quietly and deeply religious, yet inclined to be scathingly critical of others. She also was dyslexic, which may have contributed to a feeling of somehow being inadequate.

Different as they were, these two women reacted to our marriage plans with variations on a theme: Dan's mom thought I wasn't good enough for him while my mother feared that he was too good for me. Dan was from a family that was fairly formal, all dressed for dinner and seated politely in the dining room, while I was from a casual bunch who were as likely as not to be eating sandwiches on the front steps. His family belonged to the local country club, while my family struggled to put food on the table and not infrequently bought clothes at the church rummage sale.

What saved the situation was the fact that we were crazy about each other, so we ignored the frowns and carried on. By the time we reached our twentieth anniversary, having achieved a happy medium in our life together, the mothers finally came around and tacitly acknowledged that we might make it together, after all.

At any rate, both of us passed the investigative hurdle and Dan was contacted again. Now CIA requested that he spend three days at an office in suburban Virginia. He had a physical exam, a psychological exam and— saving best for last— his first polygraph, otherwise known as a lie detector test.

Then it was back to the waiting game while the total picture was being evaluated. Finally, it was done and he got word that the job was his. Six months after submitting his application, he was to report to work in late May.

Trained by the Agency in its Career Trainee program, Dan spent the better part of his first year at "The Farm," the CIA training facility in southern Virginia, taking courses geared to achieving proficiency in spy craft. Along with the rest of his CT class, he learned about microdots and dead drops. He ran around cities and towns tailing people and trying to avoid being tailed. He was instructed in the art of how to go about meeting potential assets who would be willing to provide information to the United States and recruiting them as foreign agents.

During the Cold War era of forty years ago, he took the "Crash-Bang" courses— particular favorites among the CTs— in which he learned about the finer points of explosives, the use of automatic weapons and the ultimate in defensive driving.

He even went through jungle training, an interesting exercise that paralleled his past experience as a survival instructor in the Air Force. When he returned from that particular course he was draped in a cloud of unwashed odor so strong it took several showers to dispel. That homecoming doesn't rank as one of my personal favorites.

The one course he decided to forego was the one that had CTs jumping out of airplanes in the dead of night, hoping to land in small cleared fields outlined by flickering lanterns. As it turned out, he never needed that sort of proficiency, anyway.

In the end, when his CT program drew to a close, Dan decided that his interests, skills and personality were not best suited to a career as a traditional secret agent, known otherwise as a case officer. He opted, instead, to become an administrative officer and thereafter his training was within the Agency's cadre of Management Generalists. With his expertise covering the fields of finance, logistics, personnel and support for secret operations, he emerged as a managerial jack-of-all-trades.

Not all CIA personnel sent abroad are actual spies. The case officers are there, certainly, and they are the major players, but at every station, base or installation there is at least one person, if not a whole group, providing support for the entire mission. And that's how Dan was involved.

Once he was into his job at an overseas CIA station, Dan arranged for airline tickets for those either traveling on temporary assignments or permanently changing posts. He assisted with housing leases for new arrivals and passed along local insurance information and regulations regarding the shipping of cars and household effects. And he helped untangle the confusion in pay that seemed to be an integral part of an overseas move.

But the majority of his time was taken up by the needs of the station and supporting current and ongoing operations. Periodically, the CIA offices needed to be renovated or relocated and the updating of computer equipment sometimes turned into a major project, so he and the support staff coordinated such work, arranging for outside contractors to do specific jobs. And they set up schedules for the escorts, people assigned to keep an eye on non-security-cleared workers in the restricted and classified space of the station.

Dan also located, leased and furnished safe houses, quarters used for clandestine meetings between case officers and the "assets" they managed. Sometimes the aptly named safe houses were temporary hiding spots for agents who were either defecting to the United States or on the run from danger.

He bought, sold and saw to the servicing of the station's operational vehicles and took care of shopping for items needed for secret projects. At times large equipment was required by an operation and he arranged for it to be trucked or flown into or out of the country. Frequently he had to go to the local airport, even in the middle of the night, to oversee the unloading of a large transport plane. Sometimes he slept on board, as part of a guard detail, while the crew stayed the night at a local hotel where they could get a comfortable rest.

At most posts he kept the books for the office, accounting for all monies used. Large portions of each station's budgets went toward payments to the agents who were providing requested information and services, as well as expenses for secret operations the case officers were mounting against specific targets. It often was a complex, high finance project, involving millions of dollars.

Through it all, Dan took the CIA mandate for secrecy very seriously and his work rarely followed him home. There were a few exceptions, however.

◄○►

One time the station undertook a covert project against a particularly troublesome foreign organization. To accomplish the operation, the idea was to dig a tunnel from the basement of a house, burrowing beneath a very large yard and brick wall, then under a second expanse of grass and tidy flower beds, ending directly under the building housing the group's headquarters.

A special crew was flown in to do the job and work began. As it progressed, the walls of the tunnel had to be reinforced to prevent collapse. The workers used a special foam to line roof and walls. When it dried it was light in weight, only a few inches thick, and extraordinarily strong. As the tunnel lengthened, the team had to install a lighting system and an oxygen supply, so it was an ambitious and complex operation.

Meanwhile, they had to dispose of the dirt they were excavating as well as the excess foam they produced. The blobs of hardened foam ranged from fist-sized pieces to ones that were roughly the size of watermelons. They were fascinating to look at and hold because of the queer shapes they assumed as they dried. Their qualities of being so lightweight yet incredibly strong were unusual, to say the least.

I had never seen anything like it before which, of course, was the issue the digging team had to consider. The trash collectors of that particular city hadn't ever seen anything like it, either. The crew couldn't just throw the pieces of foam into the garbage and assume that no one would be curious about it and perhaps try to find out where it came from— and why.

So, in the early days of the project, the team filled shopping bags and small boxes with the bits of foam. One by one, in trips that formed no sort of pattern, they carried the foam out of the tunnel and away from the house. The foam was loaded into a panel truck that was parked on a nearby side street, but moved periodically to avoid curiosity about its presence.

At the time, we were living several miles away in a house situated at the end of a dead-end street. Tall brick walls surrounded the lot and an eight-foot-high wooden gate closed off the driveway entrance. We were about as secluded as a residence in an urban setting could be.

The original idea of the case officers running the operation, along with the tunneling team, was to try to burn the foam. But where? They decided that our property was a perfect location, a logical choice. So the panel truck arrived at our house with its curious cargo and the foam was unloaded into our garage.

The crew was eager to complete the operation and they wanted to return to the tunnel as quickly as possible. Since I was on the spot and appeared to have nothing better to do, they requested my assistance. I agreed to become a temporary "pyrotechnic specialist." And so, shortly after they drove away, I began trying to torch the stuff.

Using a large oil drum as an incinerator, I gathered wood and paper and built a satisfactory little fire. Then I started tossing pieces of foam into the blaze. Whoa, Nellie! Spectacular flames shot skyward in bright red and yellow bursts of explosive energy. Jumping back, I watched as equally spectacular thick, black, noxious smoke billowed into the air and rose above the roof of the house. Since the idea was to dispose of the foam without attracting attention, the burn plan obviously was doomed. So, scratch that. Scratch, also, my fleeting personal involvement with a clandestine operation.

At least the garage was an ideal collection spot for the dross, so delivery runs between the tunnel and our house continued. In the end, the team just packed the pieces of foam into boxes and had Dan ship it all back to Washington. Someone there could figure out what to do with it.

Meanwhile, the crew took another look at our place, this time as a disposal site for the dirt being emptied out of the tunnel. They noted the long gravel driveway, the small grape arbor, several spacious rose beds behind and alongside the garage, and the kitchen garden plot out by an unused hen house.

The digging team copied a clever idea from the movie "The Great Escape," the one where the prisoners worked at getting rid of the dirt from their tunnel. Our crew wore special vests and pants fitted with oversize pockets, which they filed with dirt, and they piled more into boxes and sturdy canvas shopping bags. Then they came in the panel truck and proceeded to walk around the yard and through the flowers, spreading the dirt in such a way that it was virtually unnoticeable. Even the kids, who roamed the yard daily, never spotted it.

The whole operation was fascinating. Recognizing my own inherent curiosity, I'm still amazed that I didn't bombard Dan with probing questions about what was going on. But knowing that there were things he just wouldn't talk about, I didn't press the issue. That didn't stop me from listening to the crew as they came and went, however, and over time it was possible to add everything up and piece the details together.

Eventually the team stopped coming to the house— and life went on. It was years before I learned the outcome of the project. While the construction of the tunnel was a success, the real object— the covert action lying at the end of the tunnel— didn't work and ultimately the whole thing was abandoned.

◄○►

Although we always described our life as "Foreign Service," our association with the Department of State was simply a matter of Dan's cover.

The mission of the CIA is to find out what it can about situations in the world that affect, or have the potential to affect, our country, our alliances and our national security. Obviously, not all needed information can be gathered by looking at photos taken by satellites or by reading magazines and newspapers or even by watching CNN. The Agency simply has to send a certain number of people throughout the world to collect information first hand.

The Agency generally doesn't suggest to its employees who go overseas that they openly admit they are CIA personnel. Still, there has to be a credible reason for their presence in a given country. So false jobs, or diversionary positions, are created for them. Detailed cover-up stories are concocted to conceal their intent, activity and Agency association. The stories are meant to give the agents a point of departure from which they can start weaving their webs of deception. Gives them an answer, too, when someone at a cocktail party asks, "So, where do you work? What do you do?"

Sometimes an employee's cover is in the field of private industry. He or she is set up with a job as a travel agent, an exporter, an accountant or consultant. The position can be a one-person operation or within an overseas office of a large U.S. corporation. These deep-cover case officers travel with regular tourist passports and live and behave as though they are private citizens with no ties to the U.S. government. Within the Agency, they are known as non-official cover personnel, or NOCs.

NOCs differ from the usual case officers. Because they operate alone, isolated and insulated from other overseas Agency employees, they lead a difficult and dangerous life. They operate in other than diplomatic circles, in a world where they can meet those with information about industrial and computer espionage, nuclear proliferation, terrorism and drug trafficking.

While most NOCs regard their situation as invigorating and fascinating, their jobs nevertheless are stressful and full of extra challenges. They carry the workload of their cover employment while meeting the obligations of their CIA assignments. They need their own secure communications and a safe means of maintaining highly classified files. If they ever are caught, they have no diplomatic immunity. Indeed, NOCs are a special breed.

A few cover positions are created within the Department of Defense. Such covers provide case officers a legitimate government connection and include related support services afforded genuine employees of the Department.

But, up to now, anyway, most Agency personnel who serve abroad do so under cover of the Department of State, in positions within U.S. diplomatic missions. Generally, those Agency employees serving in the local CIA station or base announce themselves to the outside world as State Department officials. In all honesty, it's usually not a very good cover.

Surprisingly, some of those intended to be undercover CIA officers are recognized as Agency personnel not only by fellow Americans and foreign nationals associated with an embassy, but also by many in the communities where they serve. At two different posts real estate agents, who were driving us around town to look at available properties, pointed out the homes of the chief of station and deputy chief of station, like tourist sites. They even announced their names to us. So much for being under cover.

There are a few case officers, however, who operate with diplomatic cover stories that set them apart from their colleagues in the main office. Often, even those who work in the embassy aren't aware of their CIA connection, so their covers *do* work.

For all of these people who serve under diplomatic cover, the idea is for them to be seen as actual State Department employees. Working under diplomatic cover provides the officer an environment in which he is in a position to meet officials of foreign governments, political figures, business leaders and others who have influence within the country in question. Such cover offers the Agency representative a built-in support system which may assist in professional activities and personal needs, including secure communication facilities for use in sending and receiving messages between the overseas post and Headquarters back in the States. And, in extreme situations, diplomatic immunity is available to protect the officer if something goes terribly awry.

How did Dan fit into all this? In every post at which he served he was part of the CIA station, working under minimal State Department cover. As was the case with many others, he wasn't hidden very well. At one point Philip

Agee, disgruntled ex-CIA case officer, began a campaign to undermine and limit the effectiveness of the Agency by exposing names of covert employees. Dan was listed in two of his books.

By his treacherous actions, Agee damaged the morale of the intelligence community. His betrayal, which affected not only those specifically named but also their co-workers and spouses, was both infuriating and scary. On first learning of the situation, I was concerned for Dan's safety and, reflecting an Agency-wide reaction, angry and full of contempt for the traitor. I carry those emotions with me to this day, but Dan's stability and common-sensical suggestion that we simply stay alert acted as a calming oil on whatever dark thoughts I had and eventually worry died its own death in the face of routine.

—◦—

As dull as it may seem to those on the outside looking in, our experiences did not totally revolve around daring, dramatic cloak and dagger exploits. While it was sometimes fun and always interesting to be on the periphery of CIA activity, as a family we usually weren't involved. After all, we were trying to live under State Department cover. Most of the time we just *were* a State Department family.

Back in the old days, which is to say prior to 1972, Foreign Service wives were considered an extension of their husbands. The ideal wives were elegant, witty, multilingual, accomplished cooks and deferential mates. They were expected to be well-dressed, well-spoken, well-mannered diplomatic representatives. All without pay or recognition, of course.

An unofficial policy existed regarding "volunteerism" which was officially enforced. Incredibly, a wife's contributions or non-cooperation routinely were noted in her husband's fitness reports or professional evaluations. In addition, wives found themselves locked into a rigid hierarchy based on the ranks of their husbands.

It was an unfair situation for us to be used and judged and required to donate so much of our lives to our husband's careers. But in January 1972, things changed. A directive was issued by the Department of State and cabled to every U.S. embassy and consulate throughout the world.

The "Policy on Wives" included statements declaring that the wife of a Foreign Service employee who has accompanied her husband to a foreign post is a private individual; she is *not* a government employee. The Foreign Service has *no* right to levy any duties upon her and the U.S. government has *no* right to insist that a wife assume representational burdens.

From that point on, participation by wives in official functions became strictly voluntary. And fitness reports were limited to the husbands' work performances.

But when we began our overseas experience, the old order was still in force. Upon arrival at a post Dan made his rounds, meeting section heads and fellow staff members, as part of his check-in procedure. Like other newly arrived wives, I was expected to make social calls on the wives of ranking officers, including the ambassador's wife.

Once settled, wives were virtually required to join the wives club and to make ourselves available for representational duties. We also were at the beck and call of ranking wives. Just as a section head wielded power over those in his department, too often his wife wanted control over the spouses of those staff members.

Sometimes a large cocktail party was scheduled at the ambassador's residence or the home of a senior official and the call went out to the "drone wives." We were summoned to a meeting where the resident "dragon lady" issued assignments: "You are scheduled to be here from 6:30 to 7:30 on Saturday evening. You will provide four dozen canapés and you are expected to carry your tray from group to group, making polite conversation with the guests. Please wear a basic black dress and appropriate shoes."

Treated more as servants than guests at such social functions, we were not encouraged to discuss the fact that these required services were demeaning.

One ambassadorial spouse declared that no diplomatic wife was to wear green to an upcoming event since *she* planned to wear green that evening. Another regularly called on junior wives to do her grocery shopping.

One time the doorbell at our home rang and there stood a senior wife I barely knew. She explained that she was on her way to buy a wedding gift but realized she had no cash in her purse. Since she was near our house, she stopped to get money from me. She didn't ask for a loan, nor did she apologize for the unexpected request. She simply stated that she wanted a specific amount.

Totally surprised, and like a ninny, I handed over that week's grocery money. Several weeks later I had to contact her husband to arrange to be repaid.

At one post, we encountered the wife of the embassy administrative officer, a woman who was in her glory, finally having her day. Along with her husband, she had climbed the rungs of the diplomatic ladder and had paid her dues. Her name was Paulette and she claimed all junior wives as her personal social servants. She held monthly meetings at her house and was bitingly insistent that we attend those meetings— and be on time!

At the meetings she laid out her thoughts on current volunteer projects around the city we "ought" to organize or become involved in. Tellingly, Paulette herself was much too busy overseeing us to volunteer her time elsewhere. She happily assigned our duties for upcoming representational events, frequently ordering us to help set tables for luncheons or dinners to which we were not invited. And she constantly reminded us about proper behavior in public. No matter what we did, or when or where, it always reflected the government of the United States of America and we weren't to forget it! It wasn't a bad message, really, but her constant preaching was somewhat counter productive.

After the meetings at Paulette's house, we young wives adjourned to Ann's home nearby and good-naturedly complained about our self-appointed general and her attempts to mold us into perfect diplomatic wives. Her efforts to whip us into shape were successful, despite herself. Because we had so much fun together, forming bonds of affection and friendship that endure to this day, we did Paulette's bidding and learned some useful lessons in tact, generosity and consideration for others.

There was only one time I rebelled and openly objected to silly, unreasonable demands in the game of diplomatic etiquette. Within four days of our arrival at one post, both Penn, then two, and Sam, ten months, developed meningitis and were hospitalized. In the midst of the crisis, the ambassador's social secretary managed to track me down by telephone at the hospital. Unbelievably, she pointed out that to date I had failed to pay my call on the ambassador's wife.

She really got my back up. Full of immediate indignation, I flashed back, "Since you called the hospital to speak to me, you have to know about our problem. You should be ashamed of yourself." The social secretary never phoned again with her reminder and I never made a call on that ambassador's wife.

Apart from that incident, we can think of few negatives in our association with the State Department. By being integrated into the official American community through the circumstances of our cover, we gained much. We were exposed to wonderful experiences and were privileged to participate in events otherwise unavailable to us.

◄o►

But back to being on the periphery of CIA activity.

Years ago the OSS (Office of Strategic Services, predecessor of the CIA) developed a liquid chemical called "Who, Me?" It was terrible stuff. When ingested, it caused its victim to exude a most horrible body odor, similar to a concentrate of garlic-breath, through every pore. While it was intrinsically harmless, its effect was unbelievably repulsive and lasted for several days.

Although it is no longer featured in the Agency's arsenal, the idea behind its use back then was to prevent or sabotage a meeting between two parties or to take a person out of action by temporarily removing him from the social scene. Anyone suffering the affects of "Who, Me?" was not fit company for man or beast.

In its immediate base form it was nearly odorless and tasteless, and a clever case officer could administer a dose to the target by adding a few drops of the concoction to his drink at a cocktail party or to his beer at the local pub. Within a few hours, the victim was a walking poster child advertising the horrors of terminal halitosis and BO. No one— repeat, *no one*— could stand to be around him.

For some reason, one station was sent a supply of "Who, Me?" but apparently no one chose to pollute the pristine environment of the high-altitude post by using the vile fluid. So, by the time Dan arrived on the scene, six little vials still sat in their special container on a shelf in the supply room.

During a period of updating inventory records, Dan took another look at the "Who, Me?" supply. "What is this stuff?" he asked. "Is anyone going to use it? Is there any need to keep it on hand any longer?"

The chief pondered the questions, then replied, "Get rid of it."

Right. Actually, it was easier said than done. Dan couldn't pour it down the drain in the men's room. The chief would frown on having to close the office for the rest of the week due to unexplained odor. He couldn't toss it in the garbage and risk some poor innocent getting his hands on it. Finally, Dan and his colleague Bob decided to take it out in the country— *way* out in the country— to dispose of it. They invited me along for the ride.

Dan, Bob and I headed north out of town. We drove a couple of hours, simply to put distance between the Americans and any scent of questionable origin. At last we stopped and Bob balanced the vials, one by one and very carefully, on a large flat rock twenty feet off the deserted dirt road. Then he and Dan took turns shooting at them with a pistol. The explosions caused the glass to vaporize and the droplets of "Who, Me?" fell like mist onto the scrub grass behind the rocks.

Just out of curiosity, we waited ten minutes or so. Any faint hint of garlic that might have been in the air quickly drifted away in the soft breeze. As we got back into the car to return home, we saw, heading toward us over a small hill to our left, a shepherd and his herd of sheep.

The guys could hardly warn the shepherd to keep his animals away from the area, so we just drove away. And all the way back to town we wondered how fate dealt with the Indian and his wooly companions. Did any of them nibble at that grass? The mental image of *really* stinky sheep kept recurring and, time and again, one or another of us burst into laughter as we rode along.

◄○►

One day, about mid-morning, Dan drove into our driveway with two companions. They parked and closed the gate behind them. I knew Jack, a small and tidy case officer whose wife was my good friend, but the other man was a stranger. He was a hunk— tall, handsome and athletic, with hair the color of an Irish setter. Dan introduced him as Nick and explained that they needed to do some work on Nick's car. I asked no questions and left them to their work.

By noon they finished their project and came inside to wash up. I fixed sandwiches for all of us and, as we sat together having lunch, we enjoyed a spirited conversation. Nick was funny and kept us laughing at his quick-witted comments. It was a pleasant interlude, but soon the threesome went on their way.

I gave no further thought to the meeting. The next week Dan and I went out for dinner at a restaurant in town and there was Nick. Accompanied by a woman, probably his wife, they were seated across the room with another couple. As Dan and I made our selections from the menu, Nick's party finished their meal and stood up to leave.

To reach the door, they had to pass next to our table. Dan saw my eyes light up in recognition and also saw me take a breath, obviously ready to say something like, "Well, hello there, Nick. How are you?"

Shielded by the table, Dan suddenly stomped on my foot as hard as he could. The unexpected action was effective. It immediately diverted my attention. As I looked at Dan with a wounded expression and asked, "Why did you do that?" the two couples left the restaurant.

When the door closed behind them, Dan began his apologies. First, he apologized for stomping on my foot. He hoped he hadn't hurt me, but he had to keep me from speaking to Nick. Next, he apologized for not having clued me in.

Nick was serving under deep cover as a businessman representing an international company. He was a NOC who had contact with the station only on rare occasions. The reason the threesome came to our house was to work in complete privacy as they installed a concealment device in his car, allowing him to carry papers and documents in a nearly undetectable secret space.

Dan forgot to warn me: "You have never seen or met Nick. We never came to the house together."

Except for that brief visit, there was no reason for me to recognize the man or to indicate that we had ever met. Such acknowledgement could raise awkward questions.

Both Dan and I learned something from the situation. I had to become less straightforward and innocent in my approach to life. I needed to remember that there was a shadowy world that marched along next to ours. Dan had to remember that sometimes it was necessary to tell me a few details about his work, just to avoid my spilling beans I didn't know existed.

In fact, it really was okay for Dan to talk about some things to me. After all, I wasn't the enemy. I even had limited secret clearance. At two posts I worked briefly as a part-timer in the station, even though I was there with no training or even much knowledge of what the objective was.

Of course, there were times when I was curious about certain operations and what went on within the secure area of the offices where Dan worked. But the routine nature of what I saw and did when spending time at my jobs wasn't stimulating enough to propel me headlong into a pursuit of full time employment with the CIA.

The most titillating aspect of my short life as a CIA employee was being assigned my own code name, or pseudonym. I was Hannah Z. Pisposil. Great name, but she wasn't destined to become an immortal legend in clandestine adventures. Dan has a pseudo, too, but I can't disclose it; it's still classified. You know the story— if I told you, then I'd have to kill you.

It didn't really matter that Dan kept most of his Agency life separate from family life. We decided that most couples probably don't thoroughly discuss details of every workday. Just how much more can a dentist find to say about another root canal? Or how was today that much different than yesterday down at the button factory? So, what we occasionally did discuss was the CIA in general and interesting things having to do with our friends.

◄○►

Larry, a dark haired, suntanned man with a big nose and heavy spectacles, was a co-worker who arrived in town with just the clothes on his back. At his previous post, he headed an operation directed against a terrorist organization. The group learned of his interest and identified him.

One morning Larry noticed two men following him along a street in the city center. He ducked into a small passageway between shops just as a car screeched to a stop at the curb and two other men jumped out. The chase was on.

As he hurried down the narrow alley, shots were fired, striking the walls around him. Reaching a corner, he turned left and ran toward the largest department store in town, just down the street.

He dashed through the door, then up the stairs. He hid in the middle of a display of hanging rugs. Finally, he left his hiding place, found a telephone and called co-workers at the office.

Fellow case officers worked feverishly to come up with a rescue plan. No one knew whether the terrorists were searching the department store or perhaps keeping watch on the streets outside. Because Larry's identity obviously had been blown completely, he no longer could work effectively in that city. The best option was to get him out of the country as soon as possible.

With the cooperation of the store manager, two case officers became deliverymen. Larry was placed in a large carton. He was wheeled to a van parked behind the store, loaded inside, and the case officers drove him away. Airline tickets were purchased and office mates collected his passport from his safe at work. With no delay at the airport, he boarded the plane. Which is how he happened to join us in the country where we were serving.

I mention the story only because it was so unusual. Generally, Dan's co-workers did not have to literally run for their lives. Most of the time, guns weren't fired. Most of the time, work-related excitement was more benign.

—◄o►—

It was Larry who figured in a quirky little farce centered around our house about a year later. One morning I looked out an upstairs window and noticed a man leaning against a telephone pole across the street. He was a stranger, in his mid-thirties, with a bad haircut and sunglasses too small for his broad face. He didn't seem to fit in the neighborhood. I looked again a few minutes later and he was still there.

Now, the one thing we became obsessive about while living overseas was security. The best way to stay safe is to be alert. We took notice of people who might be loitering anywhere in our vicinity. We kept an eye on strange cars that parked for too long in our neighborhood or drove up and down the street too often or apparently without purpose.

When out shopping, we didn't keep our eyes downcast, looking at the sidewalk as we walked. We kept our heads up, eyes moving. We looked at people's faces and watched what was going on around us. All those actions are part of being alert. And being alert just might be enough at some point to avoid a dangerous situation.

Anyway, after looking a third time and seeing the man still leaning against the pole and casting glances at our house, I finally went to the phone. I called Dan and told him about the suspicious character.

Our house was several blocks from the nearest bus stop. We did not live on a corner, where someone conceivably could be waiting for a ride. There were no shops or stores in the area. Every house on the block was surrounded by a high fence, but the man wasn't near a gate where he might be waiting to talk to someone inside. The pole he was leaning against was in front of an unfenced vacant lot. The man was woefully out of place.

Dan recognized all those things and his advice was: "Get the camera. Take a few shots."

So I did. I found a spot at the boys' bedroom window where I could poke the camera lens behind the curtain without its being seen from the street. I snapped a couple of good close ups of the man. Before I could leave the window, however, another man caught my attention. He was walking down the sidewalk directly toward the first man. And the first man had straightened up and was stepping away from the pole.

Focusing on both men, I continued taking pictures. They approached one another, then stopped to talk. Both looked toward our house. They checked their watches. After speaking to each other again briefly, the first man walked away. His replacement then took up the post, leaning casually against the pole.

Strange. Very strange. But all of it was now recorded on film. I called Dan again and reported the peculiar development. He decided to drive home for lunch and pick up the film. He wanted to take it back to the office, have it developed and then show the pictures to some of the fellows. Maybe someone would have an idea about what was going on.

When Dan got home, the second man was still leaning against the pole. As he closed the gate, Dan paused and looked directly at the watcher, making it obvious that his presence was noted. The man ambled away. We never saw him again.

Back at work, Dan had the film developed. He then walked down the hall to Larry's office, prints in hand. He told Larry about the two men, tossed the photos on his desk and asked, "What do you make of this?"

Quickly flipping through the pictures, Larry roared with laughter. He recognized the twosome.

At that time, Larry was acting as liaison with the local police force and teaching a course to a group of policemen in surveillance techniques. The assigned activity for the students that week was to work in pairs, choose a residence— entirely at random— and observe outside activity at the house. They also were to keep an eye on the comings and goings in the neighborhood over a period of three or four hours. The idea was to keep watch without attracting attention.

Larry was delighted to have the photos. Perfect examples of what not to do, they would be the centerpiece at that week's classroom session.

Go View the Land

Her name was Rahab. Although she was from a heavily fortified city in the Middle East and I am a product of the placid, rural American Pacific Northwest, a few points of commonality link the two of us.

Somehow or other, Rahab got caught up in the shadowy world of espionage. Her active participation began when she hid two spies in her home as local authorities pressed a search for the secret agents. During that intense time, she worried about the safety of her family and feared reprisals against them.

My involvement with a life of covert activity began when I married a member of a clandestine service. Eventually only one spy sought refuge in my home, while a frantic search to learn his whereabouts was underway. But I understand Rahab's anxiety. Frankly, I was terrified that *our* spy's pathway to defection would be traced to our front door. And then what?

Although there are parallels to our stories, the details aren't mirror images and a couple of huge differences exist. Emerging from the mists of time, her story is told in the Bible, in the book of Joshua. In addition, Rahab, woman of Jericho, was a harlot.

I'm just a typical wife and mom, doing my best to keep things running, hoping that everybody stays healthy, happy and well adjusted. And, if truth be told, I'm a stranger to harlotry, having not even a nodding acquaintance with it.

Even so, I feel a kinship with Rahab. Fear filled her life during the days when she hid the spies and I relate to a stress factor that transcends a vast gulf of time, place and circumstance.

But it's not just Rahab with whom I feel a connection. There's also a link with the spies themselves who found safety in her home, I relate to their mission and to the journey they took and can understand the assignment they were given, as is recorded in the narrative which begins:

"And Joshua the son of Nun sent two men secretly
from Shittim as spies, saying, 'Go view the land,
especially Jericho.' And they went, and came into the
house of a harlot whose name was Rahab, and lodged
there."

In its own way, our government likewise said to us: "Go view the land." So we went. And we did.

◄◦►

A huge crowd, several people deep, pressed against the fence. They were standing on tiptoe and craning their necks for a better view, waving arms in friendly greeting and flashing white smiles in dark faces. As we came down the steps from the open door of the airplane, I breathed in the hot, sweet, slightly damp air of the tropical evening and wondered whom the well-mannered throng was waiting for.

Turns out it was no one in particular. With planes flying into Victoria, Curuba, only once a week, "going to the airport" was simply popular local entertainment.

We got into the staff car and began a breakneck ride into town, dodging bicyclists, ox carts and oncoming trucks as Walter, the driver, busily motioned with hands and chattered away in a happy singsong. Leaning over to Dan, I asked what language he was speaking. "It's English, Honey." And so it was that we arrived at our new home.

Tropical? Yes. Paradise? No. The place had a dilapidated look to it, where the metal roofs on many of the houses looked rusted and beaten from a losing battle with the constant humidity. Lining most of the streets were not sidewalks but smelly ditches meant to carry away excess water during the rainy season which, at other times, were stagnant ribbons of a filthy incubator system for armies of mosquitoes. The people were colorfully but shabbily dressed. Combining orange, green and purple, or stripes and plaids was not an issue. Since covering one's body was the necessity, there was no bowing to the god of fashion. And as for the common mode of transportation, the buses were of the homemade variety, basically a rectangular wooden box, painted a wilted green, faded rose or defeated blue, built atop a basic chassis and fitted with board seats, although without glass in the windows.

After making our way through all of this, my eyes opening wider in fascinated wonder at every new scene, it was with relieved appreciation when we drove at last into Fulton Court. A small, clean, residential compound located off a rather busy street not far from the cricket grounds, it was composed of seven well kept white houses with red roofs, each facing onto a central common green. The third house to the right was ours.

Now, Victoria is one of those places where people drive on the wrong side of the road from the wrong side of the car. It's also the place where, just a few months after our arrival, the major newspaper in town ran the headline: "Cannibals Invade Border Area, Lusting for Women."

And it is the place where the local defense force stored all its guns in a single warehouse. Someone broke in— and stole everything. At the time, they were involved in a border dispute with their neighbors to the south. Shortly after the theft, a picture in the newspaper showed a local soldier hurling rocks across the river at his counterpart. When you think about it, that may be the most civilized way to wage war.

The tiny country participated in the 1965 World Fair in New York. They sent a collection of colorful jungle birds to be part of their exhibit. One macaw was expelled, with accompanying horrified/delighted press coverage, for loudly and repeatedly reciting its profane vocabulary. So crude were its words that even construction workers at the exhibit blushed. The bird was sent home in disgrace, sentenced to live out its life in Victoria's zoo— where it daily performed its routine for local children.

In that hot, muggy place summer clothing was removed from display in stores in December. When a friend of ours asked for swimming suits to carry to little nieces for Christmas gifts, the saleslady explained in condescending weariness, "But, Madam, it's WINTER!"

Christmas decorations were displayed on store shelves as soon as they arrived by ship from Europe— in August. We had to hurry and buy them then because they were snapped up within a week. And no more were to be had— until the next August.

This is the place where one of our friends, who was packing up to leave the tropical post, sighed and said, "I'm not sure if I spent two years here or just one looong July." And there we were, beginning a tour of nearly three years, a time when we learned that, yes, we could cope with life in the foreign service

From the moment we stepped foot in our house, it began to dawn on me that, indeed, we had stepped into a whole new world. Dan had things ready for us. He had flown to Victoria three weeks ahead of Baby Penn and me and had unpacked our airfreight shipment and managed to put the new crib together. I thought the gauzy drape of soft, white cheesecloth arranged to hang over the baby's bed was a sweet and tender gesture. Actually, it was a practical touch. The canopy was, in reality, a mosquito net.

The house had been leased recently and we were the first family assigned to live there. While there were plans to set things right, at the moment it was in a sorry state. Big white rings of mildew speckled the red tile floor and the mesh screens covering the large open windows were torn.

Swatting at a mosquito, I caught the flash of motion out of the corner of my eye. "What in the world is that? Omigosh— it's a lizard! Look! There's another one!"

Figuring that Dan would take the hint and get busy ridding the living room of the little red-eyed reptiles, I was mildly surprised that he just sat there, smiling.

"Don't worry about them," he said. "They don't want to bother us. All they're interested in is the mosquitos. Just think of them as pets you don't have to walk or feed."

So. Adjustment number one.

After a couple of days I accepted the presence of the green geckos and began to regard them as benign little visitors. Not so the tarantula.

I was in the kitchen fixing breakfast. Opening the cupboard door under the sink, I reached for the hand towel—then leaped backward a record-setting eight feet, at least. There, staring at me, was the most enormous and *ugliest* spider I had ever seen. Its body was nearly saucer-size, maybe four inches across. The black hairy legs bent up, then splayed down and out. Altogether it would have filled a dinner plate.

My shrieking summoned Dan and he found me with my back against the far wall, holding the broom like a shield. Happily, this time he took the hint. He dispatched the tarantula while I worked at learning how to breathe again.

Curuba is home to some unbelievable creatures. Like, snakes so large that they regularly feed on dogs and pigs. One newspaper account reported a twenty-foot specimen wrapping itself around the supporting leg of a house that stood on stilts— and pulling the entire structure down.

There are colorful, poisonous frogs and deadly centipedes nearly two feet long. And tarantulas even larger than the one lurking in our kitchen. Clearly, creepy-crawlies in our new home were destined to catch my attention in a hurry.

—◦►—

Dan and I took turns closing up the house at night before going to bed.

The house featured a spacious L-shaped living room/dining room area. Lining the outside walls were four sets of double windows, seven or eight feet tall. Sturdy wooden storm shutters swung shut over the screened windows and fastened with steel shafts fitted into brackets.

On this particular night, Dan went upstairs while I stayed behind to batten down the hatches. I made my rounds, then paused at the foot of the stairs to turn out the light. I happened to glance up at the ceiling. There, hanging from a beam that ran the length of the room was— a mouse?

"Hey, Dan! Come here a minute!" I called. Having begun undressing, he returned to the living room wearing only his shorts and t-shirt. Pointing at the ceiling, I continued, "Look at that mouse. How can it just hang there?"

"That isn't a mouse," he answered. "That's one huge cockroach." It certainly was. The thing was at least three inches long. Maybe more. Dan knew I wouldn't rest—nor allow *him* to rest— until the cockroach was gone, so we set about getting rid of the monster bug.

Dan is tall, about 6'2", but the ceilings in the house were twelve feet high. He grabbed a chair and balanced it on the coffee table. Snatching the latest issue of *Time* magazine, and rolling it into a tube, he climbed up onto the chair. My job was to steady him.

Unfortunately, we didn't realize that some cockroaches can fly. Balanced on the chair, Dan drew his arm back and followed through with a powerful swing. "Thwack!" He missed. And the cockroach dive-bombed him.

Startled when it hit him in the chest, then flew away into the dining room, Dan raised both arms above his head and kicked one long leg into the air. Naturally, that upset the balance of things and there was no way I could hold the chair in place. We both went tail-over-teacup.

Surprised not only by the unexpected whir of wings but also by Dan's frantic gyrations, I sat on the floor and laughed. Big mistake. He didn't think it was so funny. "Here!" he grumped, as he slapped the magazine into my hand. He rolled a copy of the local newspaper into another tube and stomped off into the dining room.

I joined him there and we stood together, well away from any surface where the cockroach might have landed. Our eyes swept the room. Finally, Dan spotted it clinging to one of the curtains. Gingerly stepping forward, he swung again. And missed, again.

As quick as a flash, the cockroach spread its wings and flew directly toward him. It tangled its feet in the hair on one of his legs. Well. Let me tell you. I have *never*, before or since, seen a dance like the one he did then.

Lifting his knee to his chest, he kicked like an out of control Radio City Rockette. He hopped from one leg to another, then kicked some more. That cockroach never counted on such a wild ride. Bending at the waist, Dan slapped at both legs while switching between high-step and fast shuffle. It was wonderful to watch. At last, the cockroach freed itself and disappeared into the shadows.

I was still convulsed in laughter, gasping for breath, when Dan growled, "Oh, forget it! I'm going to bed!" And off he went. Unwilling to do battle on my own, I followed him up the stairs.

We found the cockroach in the middle of the kitchen floor the next morning. Dead. Apparently the cat was more successful in the hunt than we were and had left her trophy catch in a spot where we couldn't fail to see it.

◄○►

Others who hear us talk about "the maid" may think that we're showing off, but actually the addition of servants was not something we yearned for. Yet, as we were to learn, household help was a necessary part of our lives during a major portion of the time we spent overseas. Breaking and entering was a problem in Victoria and it was strongly recommended that we hire a maid for security, if for no other reason. We were cautioned to never leave the house unattended.

Getting used to having a maid around all the time was a big adjustment. In fact, the first time I encountered a maid, I was already facing a number of big adjustments. I'd never been outside the United States before, but here I was, only 24 years old and in a strange, new country. To date, I'd never had a need to establish any sort of real housekeeping routine, let alone think about overseeing someone who would do the chores for me. In addition, I was still in the throes of learning how to care for our newborn son.

At any rate, here we were. Dan flew to Victoria first, moved into the house and hired Matilda to be our maid. Three weeks later, Penn and I arrived on a Friday afternoon. The following Monday morning, Dan went off to work and left me to meet Matilda alone.

A big woman with huge shoulders and arms, she was old enough to be my mother and her brooding nature was apparent from the start. To say that she intimidated me is an understatement. Matilda had been a domestic worker for many years and knew the routine well. I, on the other hand, didn't have a clue about what was going on. I was easy-pickings for Matilda and she had me trained in no time at all.

She called me "Madam" and at first I looked around, wondering whom she was talking to. But no matter the form of address she used, she still had the upper hand. She organized our house the way she wanted it. She was so much in charge that I walked quietly in our own home and tried to stay out of her way. She talked about "her" washing machine, "her" floors, "her" house. I drew the line only when she started talking about Penn as "her" baby. It didn't matter if she wanted to adopt the vacuum cleaner or take over the kitchen, but that baby wasn't "hers." It was my joy to care for him and I wasn't about to turn him over to her.

Matilda had a thing about paper towels. She always rinsed the used ones, hung them out to dry and kept them neatly folded in a kitchen drawer, ready for re-use. Sometimes, if I wanted to live in the fast lane, I reached to pull a new one from the roll. But she kept me in line. To this day, I make sparing use of the quicker picker uppers that hang on our kitchen wall.

It wasn't an altogether sad day when Matilda announced that she was setting herself up in business as a seamstress and would no longer work for us. As luck would have it, the former maid of some neighbors had just returned to Victoria from a five-year stay in Haiti and needed a job. They recommended her highly, and so Louisa came to be our helper and friend.

Louisa was a funny little person, alert and perky like a bird. With boundless energy, she hummed her way around the house, making herself useful in a gentle way. All of a sudden, it was *my* house! Louisa let me come home! Penn adored her and crowed in delight when she arrived each morning on her bicycle, carrying the handful of tiny bananas she bought at a local market. Louisa was into voodoo— big time— but that didn't change the fact that she was a joy to have around.

Each time we had a maid, we also had a gardener, though the maids were full-time employees and the gardeners came only once a week. When Jai, whose habitual broad grin displayed even, white teeth in his handsome young face, appeared at our house in Victoria looking for part-time work, our yard was just a yard. It had grass and an assembly of uninteresting plants and bushes leaning in boredom along the length of the fence.

Jai's regular job was at the nearby national Botanic Garden and over the next two years, he transformed our yard into a place of beauty. He brought tiny cuttings from the Botanic Garden, coaxed roots and planted them. He traded some of our nondescript filler plants to other gardeners in the neighborhood for a variety of colorful crotons and arranged them near our gate. Jai had a gift, a true gardener's touch, and the yard grew lovelier by the day.

By the time we left Victoria, pink and white oleander, delicate jasmine and hibiscus plants that drooped under the weight of clusters of lovely blossoms surrounded us. Jai also performed one other service for us. With his machete, he kept the yard free of snakes. If for no other reason, he was worth having around. And all for only five dollars a week.

◄○►

It didn't take long to meet everyone on the staff there at our first post. Of the six CIA employees, two of them sported a glass eye. That was just odd enough to make me seriously wonder about the group Dan was working for.

We were assigned an embassy-leased house, next door to the chief of station's home. The man was a tangle of incongruities. Gentle, generous and a loyal friend, he looked like a stevedore, with barrel-chest and bulging biceps, big nose and large fleshy mouth. As a young man he was a classical scholar at Harvard, yet his elocution was unfortunately wanting. Like Elmer Fudd, his R's came out as W's. It can be hard to take someone seriously when they're heard to speak of "the weal Gweek twagedy . . ."

Because of the tropical heat, the chief frequently entertained guests outside on his shady veranda surrounded by hanging baskets of orchids and colorful hibiscus plants. Many of his luncheons and dinners actually were meetings with agents who were making intelligence reports to him.

His voice was the sort that carried. And when it bounced off the surface of the water in his small swimming pool, he might as well have been using a directional loud speaker aimed directly at us. As was common with houses in that tropical city, there was no glass in our windows, just mesh screens, so we often could hear much of what he was saying. For security reasons, it made sense to have us live next door to him, rather than someone not associated with the station.

At least half the time he did remember to put music on his stereo system and then turn on the outside speakers. The sound helped muffle the conversations taking place. But he invariably forgot to switch off the outside speakers when his guest departed.

Later, in the evening after such a meeting, he decided to relax, read and listen to music. He was an opera lover and, in the privacy of his living room, he cranked up the volume, ready to enjoy the glorious sound.

In the quiet of the night, the outside speakers did their job. The music really soared. Through all those mesh screens, it filled every house in the neighborhood. We came to love those moments since, in the house on the other side of us, lived Angela, a rather noisy woman who HATED opera. At the first blast, be it the overture or the chief's favorite aria, we'd smile at each other and lay our books aside. We knew what was coming.

Soon we'd hear it, the *slam* of her front door. Then, *crunch, crunch, crunch* as she stomped past our house on the gravel driveway. And, finally, "Mr. Phelps! MR. PHELPS! May I remind you— there are those of us who loathe your musical taste! Please lower the volume!" Then ... silence in the night air ... *crunch, crunch, crunch* ... *slam*!

The sequence became routine. Now, all these years later, whenever I hear opening notes of an opera, I listen for Angela's voice, "Mr. Phelps! MR. PHELPS!"

◄◦►

Penn was an infant, not quite a month old, when we arrived. He was a walking, talking little boy, big brother of Sam, when we left. In our first months in Victoria, I sometimes took Penn with me when I went to town to do my shopping. People were fascinated with his fair coloring—white blond hair and blue eyes— and they took him from my arms, just to touch him and hold him. Friendly or not, they alarmed me so I stopped carrying him along and left him home with the maid as baby sitter.

Just before Penn's first birthday, the Canadians who lived next door packed up and left for Bermuda and a family from England moved in. They were among the first in a lengthy list of colorful characters who took their places in our memory banks. John, the father, was assigned to the British embassy. Retired from the Royal Navy, he sported a full black beard and was the first man I ever knew who wore a gold loop through his ear. He also drank raw eggs for breakfast.

John's wife, Angela, was a tiny woman, wiry and hard as nails. Her curly gray hair bushed out from her head, making it look like she just stuck her finger in an electric socket. Angela was one of those people who yelled *all* the time. It sounded like a lot of fighting went on in their house, but it was only Angela hollering her way through life. She was the mother of eight sons— which might explain the screaming.

The six oldest sons were in boarding school in England so only Simon and David arrived with their parents. Both were beautiful children, but five-year-old Simon was recovering from an accident that occurred the previous year. A truck struck him and his injuries left him speaking in a droning monotone.

He even cried in a monotone. We know this because every night Simon fell out of bed. There we were, sitting in our living room reading quietly, when through the open windows came the sudden "Thump!" of Simon hitting the floor. The crash always was followed by his monotone wail, "WAAAA!"

John and Angela believed in a spartan life. They wanted to toughen up their boys so there was no coddling when Simon rolled out of bed. They didn't even bother to push a chair next to the sleeping child to help prevent his nightly tumble.

Simon and David had few toys and it wasn't long before they discovered that the American toddler next door had shelves full of colorful books and playthings. The soft knocking at the door alerted me and I opened it to find Simon standing there, with three-year-old David behind him. Taking a cue from his mother, Simon screamed in his monotone way, "ALLOLIT-TLEPENN'SMUMMY! CANPENNCOMEOUTTOPLAY?"

The boys usually paid their visits when Penn was napping, so I replied, "No, Penn is sleeping, but would you like to come in and play?" To which,

Simon beamed his beautiful smile and yelled at the top of his lungs, "YESMUM. THANKYOUVERYMUCH!" In moments the living room was a shambles as they played with every toy within their reach and happy shouts bounced against the walls.

As Penn grew taller and steadier on his feet, he did go outside to play. He was the littlest one and his English playmates coaxed him along as he started to talk.

A quick study with words, it was no time at all before he spoke in long sentences. Dan and I were pleased with his verbal skills and were glad that he spoke clearly and was easy to understand. When we returned to the States on vacation after his second birthday, he easily carried on long conversations. Gramma and Grandad were charmed. Not only was this little grandson surprisingly verbal, but he also spoke with a decidedly British accent.

Dan and I were surprised at their discovery. We hadn't recognized that Penn had an accent of any kind. We just accepted how he pronounced words and that was that. But what a funny vacation! Little cousins gathered together from Massachusetts, Virginia and Victoria and played together for the first time. And each had a strong accent: broad Boston, southern drawl and "veddy" proper English. It was a joy to just stand by and listen to them.

─◄○►─

Tea and crumpets? For some reason, we always thought of tea and crumpets as diplomatic refreshment. You know, distinguished men in gray flannel suits and women in hats and silk dresses, sitting together in an elegant room, sipping and nibbling and being served by butlers wearing white gloves. Tea and crumpets sounded, well, refined and splendid.

Not once in nearly thirty years of foreign service life did we encounter such fare. And it was only when we stopped over in England, on our way back to the States after our final tour, that we learned that crumpets are similar to what Americans think of as English muffins.

Likewise, our view of life in the foreign service wasn't always exactly on target. As we embarked on our adventure, we had some misgivings about our ability to fit in and to adapt. It sounded like such a suave, sophisticated, urbane lifestyle. Were we about to be exposed as naïve bumpkins, totally out of our element? Not knowing quite what to expect, the very first embassy cocktail party we attended was an eye opener.

There we were: innocents abroad at a *real* party with ambassadors, port-folio-possessing ministers, international businessmen. What were we *doing there*, anyway? Drifting around, catching snippets of conversation from first one group and then another, a common theme was becoming apparent. These diplomats, these people who "mattered" were talking about … diarrhea! Guess it was just a familiar malady, a common thread of experience. We used to have more meaningful conversations around the card table playing pinochle with our pals Ken and Doris back in Maryland. Hey! We can do this! We might fit in and be able to function in this new life, after all!

While there were contrasts between preconceived notions and reality, over the years we also observed a variety of natural contrasts between our posts: enormous cities and relatively small towns; modern sophisticated atmospheres and Third World backwardness; one city below sea level, another 10,000 feet in altitude (at that height, airlines require oxygen!); a variety of languages and accents. And food: it's availability and variety were always defining factors.

Grocery shopping in Victoria took some getting used to. The open-air markets were colorful. Or, described another way, appallingly smelly and unsanitary. But at least the fruits and vegetables we bought there could be washed and peeled. Yusef Ali's butcher shop was another story altogether.

It was supposed to be the best meat market in town. It didn't look like much from the outside, but then, what did I know? Along the street in front, there were no curbs or gutters, just old worn asphalt. As the traffic took its toll, the edges of the asphalt broke away, narrowing the paved portion bit by bit. By the time I first visited Yusef Ali's butcher shop, the street was a one-lane gray strip running down the center of a bed of powdery dust.

The building was a simple structure made of wide wooden planks. There were two windows, one on each side of the entrance, and neither had panes of glass. They were just large square openings that allowed light and, sometimes, a breeze to enter. To close up at night, all one had to do was swing the doors and window coverings on their hinges and click the latches into place.

Inside, on the counter, stood a scale and the old hand-cranked cash register. There also was a big heavy table, stained thick reddish brown. And on the table lay hunks and chunks of raw, sticky beef. Not a single "cut" corresponded to the identifying pictures in the meat chapter of my Better Homes and Gardens cookbook. Here, it appeared, meat was meat and patrons purchased their hunks, chunks or slices based on the size of whatever was available.

Behind the counter and table was the heart of the operation. Big steel hooks hung from the ceiling and huge pieces of meat, still dripping, dangled from the hooks. Two men hauled sides of beef from a dilapidated old truck outside. They carried the slabs through a gaping door and heaved them onto the floor. Two other workers hacked the meat apart with razor-sharp machetes, then hung the pieces from hooks.

The air was heavy with the sickening sweet smell of blood. A black layer of flies coated the sticky surface of every piece of meat. And this was the best Victoria had to offer? Fresh from the land of antiseptic Safeway stores, I found the place a little too primitive for my taste. Nothing caught my fancy that day. Thanks, anyway.

Fortunately, fresh chicken and fish were available at other markets in town. It took a long time before I bought anything from Yusef Ali. Guess it's all a matter of what you get used to and how hungry you are.

Two fairly modern food stores also kept us going, Fan Ling's Grocery and the food department connected to Holder's Department Store. We depended on them mostly for dry, packaged goods and learned to stay away from the frozen food section, except on days when a fresh delivery was placed in the freezers. Unbelievably, the freezers routinely were turned off at night in an attempt to save electricity.

In that warm climate, thawing occurred rapidly. But the store management thoughtfully laid out slatted wooden platforms along the front of the freezers so shoppers could keep feet dry when peering in to choose between refrozen ice cream and packages of increasingly smelly fish sticks.

During the first year and a half of our tour, the embassy helped organize family orders from a food supply company back in the States. With the limitation of being able to order only by case lots, we pondered how much mustard, jelly, baby food and cereal we expected to use in six month spans. We joined with friends to share case lots of vanilla extract, cans of shortening and bottles of maple syrup.

It worked initially, but eventually too many insurance claims were being filed to make the project worthwhile. The ordering was dropped when pilfered and damaged shipments became routine. They contained cases of toothpaste that looked untouched but were minus the tubes and T-bone steaks turned fuzzy and green after a series of repeated thawings and refreezings.

And so, it was back to Holder's and Fan Ling's and Yusef Ali's butcher shop.

◄○►

Just a few months after our arrival in Victoria, while still wet behind the ears, we were given tickets to attend a speech by Indira Ghandi, then the Prime Minister of India. She was making an official visit and was to address local government officials, the diplomatic corps and international businessmen working there. Feeling that such opportunities would be infrequent, at best, Dan and I were happy to attend.

As we arrived at the small outdoor site, Dan handed our tickets to an usher. He consulted a photographic display of notables who were to be seated in a special reserved section.

A new ambassador from Germany recently had arrived in town and Dan bore a striking resemblance to him. Apparently the usher made the wrong connection. He led us to seats in the front row. While we were delighted to have such prime seating, we soon began to wonder why we were placed in front of the Chargé d'Affaires (the acting ambassador) from our own embassy. He wondered at the preferential placement, too, and it wasn't long before we heard, from over our shoulders, "Psst! What are you *doing* there?"

What did he *think* we were doing? Something about his attitude struck us as comical. We knew we were low on the diplomatic totem pole, but did he believe we had strong-armed our way into possession of those seats? Was he afraid we would make rude sounds? Pick our noses? Embarrass the embassy? Or, was he so concerned about rank and position that he wanted those particular chairs for himself?

Just then, introductory remarks began and Dan was reluctant to change to other seats. So he whispered in my ear, "Relax. Enjoy."

Green and inexperienced as we were, we managed to behave ourselves. The German ambassador couldn't have done better. We got to see and listen to Indira Ghandi, up close and personal. Where we sat that day didn't really matter in the scheme of things but, because of his protest, we retain a funny memory of the look of consternation on the face of the American Chargé.

About a year later, for some reason that same city was chosen as the site for the world premiere of a major motion picture. Not all that unusual for a production of that sort to occur in Los Angeles, Paris, New York or London, but in this small South American country, a world premiere was *really* a big deal. The director, producers and several of the stars were to be on hand. An invitation to the evening's festivities was the hottest ticket in town. In fact, it was the only hot ticket available during our two and a half years in town.

As members of the diplomatic community, we were included in the list of invitees. Our good friends and neighbors Frank and Margaret also received tickets through his British company. We decided to enjoy the movie together as a foursome. Dressed in our best, we looked forward to a classy night on the town, away from our pleasant but routine lives in Fulton Court, the seven-house residential complex we called home.

At the time I was eight and a half months pregnant and sometimes uncomfortable sitting for any length of time. To help cushion my back, I carried along a small round toss pillow.

We piled into Frank's little wood-paneled Morris Minor station wagon and drove the two miles to the only real movie theater in town. Inside, we found seats in the balcony and settled ourselves. Looking around, we spotted the Prime Minister, members of Parliament and several judges on the Supreme Court. Oh! There's Michael Caine, the actor!

After a few short remarks by relevant dignitaries, the lights were dimmed. We sat back and were treated to a movie that lived up to our expectations. It was delightful and worth seeing. As it ended, house lights came up and we stood with the rest of the audience to begin our collective departure.

The four of us made our way out of our row of seats and started down the stairs. Three steps down and ... *Oh, No*! I felt the elastic on my underpants give way. As we took another step downward, the panties began to slide.

Holy cow! I couldn't just let them go! The embarrassment would be unthinkable. I also didn't want the panties to drop around my ankles and cause me to trip and fall. Instinct took over. I immediately clamped my knees together to prevent further slippage and hunkered over.

Beside me, Dan bent his head and asked with concern, "What's wrong?"

"My underpants are falling," I managed to hiss back.

Quick to assist, he put his right arm around my waist and reached down to pinch the wayward panties between his finger tips, through the fabric of my dress.

At that point, with the pillow awkwardly squashed against my side with my left elbow, I scrabbled with my own fingers to grab the other side of the still-falling panties. There! Gotcha! However, we still had to go down half a dozen steps, walk through the half-circle of the landing, then descend the final set of stairs.

Did you ever try to go down steps with your knees glued together? Talk about ungainly progress! With each step, the funnier it got. As Dan and I sashayed slowly downward, I began to shake with silent laughter.

All of a sudden we became aware of people staring at us, noticing that something was amiss. Since the young woman was obviously well along in pregnancy and the gentleman was providing some serious support, they understandably jumped to the wrong conclusion. The concern showed in their faces.

At that, it became even funnier. I turned my face into Dan's shoulder as tears of laughter began to squeeze out of my eyes. There was a subtle change in the murmur of voices around us and I looked up to see that people were moving aside, trying to clear the stairway.

Then, through an opening in the crowd, we could see coming toward us, like characters in some bizarre dream, two members of the Prime Minister's ceremonial guard. Dressed in black pants, snow white jackets with gold epaulets and bright red sashes, the guards presented themselves to us and, opening a pathway down the stairs to the lobby, they began to escort us through the gathering of Who's Who in Victoria.

Dan managed to grab car keys from Frank as I gulped some shaky breaths for composure and muttered, "Now look here, Self. Get a grip! Stop laughing and don't let those panties fall now!" The center of considerable attention, we gingerly minced the rest of the way down.

Undoubtedly assuming that we wanted to head directly to the hospital, one of the guards accompanied us right to the car. Dan unlocked the doors and I fell into the back seat, finally letting go in great whoops of laughter.

◄o►

Dan spent one day culling office files with a co-worker. They gathered outdated and unnecessary papers and stacked them in piles ready for the burner. This was back in the days before shredders were part of routine office equipment and disposing of classified files meant hand-feeding them into an incinerator where they were reduced to ashes.

Dan and Phil began the burning early in the afternoon. About fifteen minutes into their chore, the young General Services Officer, whose office was downstairs, opened the door of the third floor room where they were working and held out a piece of paper.

"Does this belong to you?" he inquired.

Dan took the paper from Charlie and looked it over. Seeing the pseudo of the chief of station on the signature line, plus the words "CLASSIFIED – SECRET" typed at the top of the page, made his blood run cold. It definitely came from an office file.

"Where did you get this?" Dan urgently asked.

"I was just coming back from lunch," Charlie replied, "and it was lying on the sidewalk outside."

Dan looked at the page again and recognized it as one of the papers chosen to be burned that day. How had it ended up outside on the street?

Quickly, Dan and Phil checked the remaining files and soon determined that the paper Charlie returned to them was one they had already fed into the incinerator.

"What's going on here?" they wondered.

It didn't take long to figure it out. A screen fitted at the top of the chimney, specifically designed to keep all solid matter confined, had given way. After years of use, it finally burned through and that afternoon, as Dan and Phil fanned the flames and began tossing in page after page, a strong updraft carried pieces of paper up and out.

Anyone standing around looking at the station's roof that day would have seen an unusual sight. At the Vatican, puffs of gray smoke or white smoke issuing from the chimney signal results of votes for a new Pope. In Victoria, the Americans were sending a flurry of documents into the air. Maybe they were electing a new Congress or something?

Dan and Phil rushed down the stairs and spent the next hour hurrying around several blocks adjacent to the station, peering under cars and up into trees, out in the streets and even in back yards. They collected about a dozen wayward pages, then returned to the office, hoping all had been retrieved.

◄o►

We found so much that was different and fascinating during our first overseas tour that I sent out letters to friends or family almost daily. Having Sam, then, was an experience really worth writing home about.

Five months into the pregnancy, I went to the doctor for a routine check up. He startled me to the core when he commented, "You know, I think you might be expecting twins."

Touching my belly, he said, "See, here's one head and here's another. Whoops. There it goes. They really are active ones. You're not very big yet, but they'll grow."

Wanting confirmation, I nevertheless agreed with the doctor that x-rays should be delayed until nearer the delivery date. Meanwhile, Dan and I discussed the possibility of having two babies and how it would affect us. All things considered, we thought we could handle it fairly easily, especially since we had our wonderful day maid Louisa to help out.

Both of us were pleased, particularly Dan, who had younger twin brother and sister back home in Maryland. He knew what fun a twosome could add to the family. We wrote to grandparents with the happy news.

At following checkups, the doctor continued to identify bumps and bulges as heads or rumps. He never could pinpoint positions for long, though, because of the constant somersaulting going on inside me. In addition, he never was able to hear two heartbeats but explained that, with so much activity by the two babies, it wasn't unusual.

We got used to the idea of twins and started talking about names. Two girls, two boys, or one of each? We discussed ordering extra baby furniture, but put it off for the time being. Maybe we could get another high chair locally, later. And, at first, the babies could share a crib.

About two weeks before the "big day" the doctor called for x-rays at last. I still wasn't very bulky as mothers of twins tend to be, but he wasn't concerned. With all the activity of the two, they certainly were thriving.

An x-ray was taken and the nurse developed the film while I waited in the doctor's office. She brought the film to his desk and waited as he checked it over. He immediately exploded. "There's only one baby here. What did you do? How did you mix up two films?"

The nurse tried to explain that she followed all procedures correctly. This was the right x-ray. The doctor remained unconvinced and finally sent me back for a second x-ray.

Again waiting in his office, my heart fell as the nurse returned, tentative and unsmiling, with the second film. No doubt this time. Only one baby.

A delightful, caring man with no pomposity, the doctor immediately apologized— both to the nurse and to me. He said he had never been so fooled by a baby before. This was an exceedingly active child. The "heads" and "rumps" must have been elbows, knees and feet pushing as hard as they could as the baby went through his energetic workouts.

I was so sad. Even though we had experienced one miscarriage, we always felt that that baby wasn't meant to be born. We didn't suffer prolonged or excessive grief. But this baby, the twin who never was, seemed to have been healthy and active. We were only two weeks away from welcoming him or her. Strange, but to this day I still miss that child and wonder who it would have been.

On the day Sam finally arrived, it was just about time for Dan's office to open for business when he drove me to the clinic. I preferred a private room, so we were escorted to the "luxury suite." It was made up of three rooms. First was an anteroom completely filled by two overstuffed chairs. If visitors occupied the chairs, their knees would touch. There were no windows and the cheerless color scheme featured walls painted mushroom brown with upholstery fabric of gray, black and olive green on the chairs. Right away I knew I'd be content to spend my time in the bedroom.

Actually, it was an inviting place, large and airy with big windows across one wall. On the second floor, it looked out over lush tropical trees— flamboyant, breadfruit and mango. Relaxing. Comfortable. And there was a modern bathroom with newly installed fixtures, all bright pink. Interesting that the water pipes for the bathtub weren't hooked up yet. The nurse left me speechless when she offered that "whenever you desire to have a bath, let us know and the staff will carry fresh, hot water up to you."

Once the admission process was completed and I was safely tucked into bed, Dan had to leave. The Vice President of the United States was arriving in town that morning and, with a limited number of people available for security assistance, Dan was a necessary player. He was torn about leaving but I felt fine. "Just come back as soon as you can," I requested.

He did return, just before noon. Right about then, the doctor stopped in, as well. He was on his way to have lunch in his office, but Dan's presence offered an opportunity to enjoy some conversation while dining. The doctor put a brown bag on the bed near my feet and pulled out a sandwich. And launched into a funny story.

There I was, in labor, and those two guys were telling jokes! Back and forth they went, until Dan looked at his watch. "Oops. Have to run, Honey. I'll be back in a couple of hours. You okay?"

The doctor was perfectly happy with my progress. Before following Dan out of the room, he reached up to a shelf and brought down a silver colored bell with a wooden handle. "Here. When you think the baby is coming, just ring this."

This whole approach to having a baby was so relaxed, so natural, so much *easier* than my earlier experience in Maryland when Penn was born. There, Dan was restricted to the waiting room and I was stuck in a tiny sterile cell with only a large clock on the wall for company. Here in Victoria, the situation was so casual I couldn't help but laugh as the doctor left.

About an hour later, I knew the baby was on its way. I rang the bell and into the room came two smiling orderlies who acted as though the occasion were the happiest event of their week. They pushed a gurney next to the bed and one of them lifted my shoulders as the other grabbed my feet. "One, Two, Threee," they chanted— and they swung me onto the gurney.

Away we went, down the hall, then right through the lobby. It was visiting hours, so the room was full. Progress was slow, and friendly faces smiled at me. Hands reached out to pat my arms. "Have a lovely baby, Madam." "God bless you, now." Ah, who could resist the warmth of those well-wishers?

So, he arrived. Just one baby. He looked just like his older brother with blond fuzz on little round head and eyes as blue as the tropical sky. He was so sweet and special, one of Sam would be enough.

The day after he was born, we learned about a local regulation that stipulated that new mothers and their babies had to stay in the hospital for ten days following the birth. Ten days!! Presumably that offered time for the mothers to rest and recuperate before resuming busy lives. But— ten days?

After one day, I felt great and began lobbying the doctor to authorize an exemption to the ten-day regulation. However, tiny Sam was jaundiced and needed to stay in the hospital to be monitored. By the second day, the doctor suggested a satisfactory, and workable, solution. I was allowed to go home for lunch and dinner every day!

On his way home at noon, Dan stopped at the clinic to collect me. Back at the house, we gave Penn his lunch, played with him for a while, then put him down for his nap. Then I took a shower. At least our bathtub had running water. Leaving Louisa as baby sitter, we returned to clinic and station. We repeated the routine at dinnertime.

Every night, after Dan drove me back to the luxury suite, the two of us sat cross-legged on opposite ends of the bed with the adjustable meal tray between us. While we played Yahtzee for hours on end, an orderly came around with welcome evening snacks. We enjoyed milk shakes and a variety of fruits and cakes, all meant to keep up the strength of the "little mother." Ten days wasn't so bad, after all.

―◦―

A day or two after taking Sam home, we had to register his birth. The process wasn't accomplished through the clinic so we needed to present ourselves to the registrar of vital statistics in the city district where he was born.

Address in hand, we located the house cum office. Typical of other residences in town, the white structure was raised off the ground by a foundation of stilts. Slatted shutters jutted out from the screen-covered windows, providing shade from the relentless tropical sun. Croton bushes grew in profusion along the walkway and twisting vines braided themselves up the railing along the stairs.

We climbed the steps and knocked at the door. The registrar answered our summons. Standing no more than five feet tall, she weighed at least three hundred pounds. And she was wearing a sleeveless green nylon nightgown and shower thongs on her feet. Taken aback by her unexpected attire, we started to apologize for intruding on her morning. But she flashed a beautiful smile of welcome and threw open the door, gesturing us inside.

She ushered us to her "office" which obviously doubled as dining room table. We presented a paper obtained from the clinic and explained that we wanted a birth certificate for our new son. She opened a cupboard and withdrew her necessary supplies. Desk blotter, large parchment-looking document, old-fashioned pottery ink well and an honest-to-goodness quill pen. She arranged them on the table, placing each. item. just. so.

Asking pertinent questions, she began to fill in the document. Father's name, birthplace, birth date, current address, all the necessary information.

42

Then the same for the mother. In an almost calligraphy-like script, she *drew* every letter, every stroke. She dipped the nib into the ink with a swish and a flourish as she established a snail-paced rhythm. It took *forever*!

Dan and I looked at each other and rolled our eyes. We shifted in our chairs, re-crossed our legs and tapped fingers and feet. There was no hurrying this process. We simply had to endure the wait

At last she finished. After attaching a foil seal, she rolled the certificate into a scroll and tied it with a ribbon. We paid her the required fee and beat feet down the stairs, back to the car. Free at last!

On the drive back to the house, I unrolled the scroll to look at the masterpiece. Impressive. A fitting document for the very first "official" American baby born in Victoria. But … *no*! Please, *no*! In the space reserved for the legal name of our newborn, she put the *wrong name*!

Actually, she had all the letters right. She just scrambled them. Instead of *Blake*, she wrote Sam Taylor *Labek*! I shrieked while Dan practically pounded his head against the steering wheel. The ordeal had lasted over two hours! And now we had to go through it again!

We turned around and, with dragging feet, climbed the steps once more. As before she ushered us through the door with a beaming smile, still wearing her nightgown. "Oh, dear. I am so very sorry. We must correct the error," she said in her lilting Caribbean accented English.

She retrieved desk blotter, quill pen and ink well. Placing the items on the table again just so, she added a small round clay pot full of fine sand. Sighing in resignation at the thought of spending most of the afternoon watching her draw the words again, we were surprised when she placed the original document in the center of her blotter. Squaring it to some unseen reference point, she finally had it perfectly aligned.

She picked up the feathered pen, dipped its tip into the ink well and, with a snap of her wrist, shot a blob of black ink onto the paper. Splot! It covered, exactly, the erroneous Labek. Quickly, she grabbed the pot of sand and dashed it across the surface of paper and ink. Perfect, natural blotter. She smiled at us as we waited the minute it took for the absorbing agent to do its work. Then she funneled the sand back into the pot and blew the remaining dust off the paper.

Slowly, deliberately, she drew Blake onto the page. Our son was now officially, correctly named: Sam Taylor (*Splot*) Blake.

Maybe that was a sign of how he would develop. Maybe that's where his not-quite-warped, but definitely, delightfully eccentric sense of humor came from.

◄○►

Back in the days of European exploration and colonization, possession of the entire northeastern shoulder of South America shifted among the Dutch, British, Spanish and French. Explorers from each of the empires searched for riches to claim in the name of their sovereigns. Not only did they examine the land along the coast, but they also penetrated as far as they could into the interior regions.

They traveled the rivers, among the largest of which was the Irupana. Broad and deep at its mouth, it stretches back all the way into Brazil. Control of the river was important to the early explorers and they set up a series of outposts along its banks.

Eventually a group of Dutch soldiers built a sturdy brick fort on a little island in the middle of the river some miles back from its wide mouth. From there they defended their claim of possession. But, as with the rest of the region, possession of the fort and the island itself shifted from Dutch to French to British over the years.

We've tried, but really can't imagine, the isolation and desolation felt by the troops who were posted there. Surely they grew crops on the island and raised cattle, pigs and chickens. Certainly they received occasional supplies from their homeland. They did what they could to "make do." But it's so in the middle of nowhere! More desolate and lonesome than South Dakota, even!

It's hot and dank and doesn't possess a breathtaking beauty. The water doesn't run clear and blue. Instead, because of the silt collected as it travels through swampy areas, the river is a muddy mix of brown and gray. There are no charming waterfalls or exciting rapids anywhere near the island outpost to add interest and personality to the region. We imagine lethargy seeping into the bones of those standing watch at the fort.

Some of them must have tried to blunt the edges of loneliness and boredom by hitting the bottle. In fact, we're pretty sure they did. All over the island, buried only a few inches under the muddy soil, were clues that pointed to some serious drinking sprees. Bottles, over two hundred years old and bearing markings that show they originated in Holland, England and France, were everywhere.

After consuming the wine, the gin and the rum, the soldiers tossed the glass containers into the jungle undergrowth. Decaying vegetation, dust and the splattering of mud during tropical rainstorms gradually buried the discarded bottles under layer after protective layer. Undisturbed by any cultivation of the land and spared the cycles of expansion and contraction of the earth during seasonal changes, there they remained in near original condition. Until shortly before we got there.

Now, we recognize that, when measured on a grand scale, the excursions we took during our years of foreign service rank as minor adventures. We know that the adventures of Jacques Cousteau in his Calypso and Sir Edmund Hillary on Mt. Everest are in a whole other class. But our excursions sure beat what we might have expected had Dan taken a job with some suburban branch of a bank in Maryland, or something.

Right now we were on a ferry in the middle of the Embaro River that flows along the western border of Victoria. Behind us we could see a collection of small boats pulled up onto the muddy riverbank next to the town's largest indoor-outdoor market. Farmers and other vendors gathered there daily, bringing their produce and wares to be sold in and around the sprawling building.

The variety of available goods was an interesting mix. Shoppers wandered the dirt-packed aisles and selected yams, chicken and fish, shoes, baskets and tires, cheap plastic toys, and bows and arrows straight from the jungle. Scattered here and there were stalls and tables where freshly mined diamonds and gold— exquisite filigree jewelry, coins from the old British Empire, and nuggets, both large and small— were on display.

On this day, however, we weren't interested in the market or what we could buy there. We were searching for something else. We were headed for Muru Island, that small piece of land in the Irupana River, on a quest for some of the old bottles.

In the years after the explorers departed, the island was never heavily populated. Even by the mid-1960s only about a hundred hardy souls made their homes there. As they cleared fields to plant their gardens and dug ditches for irrigation water, they began finding the old bottles. The settlers showed the quaint relics to occasional visitors who stopped at the island and, by ones and twos, they were carried into town.

Eventually we, meaning various ones of us in the British, Canadian and U.S. community in Victoria, learned about the old bottles. Found in an assortment of sizes, shapes and shades of green, they featured the delightful imperfection of air bubbles caught in the hand blown glass. Such bottles are now reproduced as decorative accent pieces by artisans at sites like Colonial Williamsburg in Virginia.

But these were the real thing! Actual pieces of history. We were interested in collecting a few of them to have as antique souvenirs from our stay in the country. Besides, since there wasn't much to do in Victoria, the fun of going out and finding them ourselves was an adventure we couldn't pass up.

So there we were, on a ferry in the middle of the river. Just crossing the Embaro was like jumping into Frontier Land and ahead of us we could see the little village of Vreed. Not a single street was paved. Leading away from the ferry landing, a narrow dirt road ran between a few wooden houses standing on skinny stilted legs.

Vreed wasn't entirely without charm. About half the buildings were natural weathered wood, while the others were painted white, reflecting an almost blinding light in the tropical sunshine. Breadfruit and mango trees, with their large dark leaves, grew near the houses and blossoms on the hibiscus and bougainvillea plants added splashes of color here and there. White smiles in the dark skinned faces of barefoot women and children welcomed us as our five-car caravan drove off the boat.

At the edge of town we met the "highway" to Osan, a settlement twenty miles away on the bank of the Irupana River. Not much as modern roads go, it at least provided a pathway through a sea of mud during the rainy season. Two strips of concrete, each about twenty four inches wide, stretched off into the distance, down the middle of the rutted dirt road bed.

As long as no one approached us while we drove along the highway, we had all four tires on the cement strips. When we met the occasional other vehicle, however, we chose our path carefully and pulled over so that only the tires on the driver's side rode on a solid surface.

The other tires ran along the pitted earthen rut, sometimes dipping so deep that the car tilted alarmingly. After the traffic passed, it was several minutes before we were able to find a stretch smooth enough to cross back again to use both strips.

We didn't race madly through the countryside, hair blowing in the wind. The twenty-mile trip took well over an hour. At least the leisurely pace allowed us time to check out our surroundings. Finally we were actively fulfilling the assignment to "Go view the land." Too bad there wasn't much to see. The flat land had been cleared of all native vegetation so, apart from the ditches on both sides of the road, there was only mile after mile of pineapple and sugar cane fields.

At last, dusty and weary, we arrived in Osan. Adjacent to the stelling, or pier, jutting out into the river, was a tiny outdoor market. A few vendors sat on wooden crates, displaying foot-long string beans lined up in rows on the hard packed earth at their feet. Others stood near tables and offered casaba melons and mounds of tiny sweet bananas.

What caught our attention, though, were the baskets full of fresh ripe pineapples. We reached through the swarming curtain of flies and plucked two of the fruits from the pile and handed them to the man who waited on us. With just a few swipes of his machete, he cut away the outer skin. Then with quick, sure strokes, he chopped the pineapple into big chunks and handed the pieces to us.

Ripened to pure gold, the treat was so juicy that sticky drops fell from our chins and ran down our arms. Utter ambrosia! In all the years and in all the travels, this source of joy and delight lingers in our memories as absolute perfection. Licking our lips, we each took another huge chunk of pineapple and, happily munching away, wandered to the end of the rickety little dock where Sir Pat was waiting for us.

M.V. Sir Pat was the local police boat. It also was the mail boat. Postal business for the settlements hacked out of the jungle along the river was the responsibility of the three-man crew. But as the area was backwater in every sense of the word, Sir Pat's schedule was sluggish and therefore flexible. That being the case, Sir Pat also was available for excursions up the river.

Our group of fifteen fit easily in the forty-foot craft and we relaxed as we motored along. For miles at a time, jungle growth of trees and vines waded right into the edges of the water. Then we came to clearings that revealed surprisingly pretty sandy beaches. At one spot two abandoned dugout canoes had been in place for so long that palm trees had grown up through them and now impaled the boats to the earth.

Now and again small flocks of colorful parrots came flying out of the trees and sailed over our heads on their way to the other side of the river. Easy to believe that we were nearing the interior region, where tribes of headhunting Indians roamed the jungles, oblivious to modern man moving ever closer to their world. The forty-five minute trip was over almost too soon.

Islanders had heard us coming so, when Sir Pat eased up to the dock, a young man with a monkey on his shoulder was waiting to grab the line, secure it and then help us off the boat. Standing back, smiling shyly at us, was a whole passel of cute barefoot children. Most of them sported an obvious family trait— ears that looked like little radar dishes stuck to the sides of their heads. We wondered just how interrelated the islanders were.

Grabbing our picnic hampers, we headed off toward the ruins of the fort, accompanied by the children. They hopped and skipped around us, interested in the fair skinned visitors. Since there were no cars on the island, there also were no roads, just well worn paths that led through the trees.

As we hiked the trail, we passed some of the one-room homes belonging to the islanders. They stood on the usual stilted legs and a few appeared to be reasonably sturdy. They had wooden walls and actual doors and corrugated metal roofs. Most, though, had both roofs and walls made of palm fronds and banana leaves. Blankets or pieces of cloth hung at the open doorways. The houses had a slightly familiar look, as though they had jumped right out of pictures on the pages of *National Geographic*.

We came to a clearing where the newest of only three substantial buildings on the island stood. It was made of brick and was long and narrow. Built by the British in the early 1800s, it originally was an administration building and meeting hall but now stood empty. Considering the size and temporary nature of the homes on the island, we thought it curious that none of the families had moved into the sturdy building.

We continued walking. Then, beyond the building and around a curve in the path, standing on a small rise overlooking the Irupana, we saw the old, now roofless, fort.

It was built of stone and brick and was surrounded by a tall stone wall. Originally the fort was two stories high, but the wooden floors had long since collapsed and disintegrated. The ruins now formed a hollow skeleton, the unshuttered windows it sightless eyes.

Facing the river were two cannons, one still resting in its stone mount, the other lying on the smooth firing platform. More than a dozen cannon balls were scattered about, gradually being diminished in size as the rusty surfaces flaked away.

Because the relics were still in place after more than two hundred years, we felt as though the site had not been visited frequently. It was almost like we had been handed the key to the door of a long forgotten room located at the threshold of primitive South American reaches.

We hardly had time to line our picnic baskets on a low stone wall near the cannons and begin exploring the fort when the skies opened and rain poured down. Part of our group dashed under big trees for protection, while a few of us ran through the doorway of a low brick building with an arched roof.

It was the fort's magazine, a structure where ammunition had been set aside to stay cool and dry. Now dark, empty and a little bit spooky, it provided protection even though we had to clear away gigantic spider webs to make room for ourselves.

Soon we were joined by two local boys, each about ten years old. One was carrying a huge black bat, its wings extended to nearly the boy's full arm span. We were fascinated by the ugly mammal and the boys were happy to show it to us. As we examined it, they announced that the islanders were always on the lookout for the creatures. As a matter of fact, one boy said, a bat like this one attacked his father's cow last month and the cow died.

"What kind of bat is it?" we asked.

"Ummm. A 'bampire' bat. That's it," he replied.

Brave souls that we were, we exploded out of the magazine, preferring to be cleansed by the short, tropical downpour than to stay in the cobwebby dark with a vampire bat. And we left the boy to carry the bat home to his father. Indeed, we learned later, vampire bats *are* a danger to man and beast in that region. But true vampire bats are much smaller than the fruit-eating variety we met that day.

We spent the remainder of the afternoon wandering around the island, wading in muddy ditches and poking into the mire with long sticks, hoping to feel a telling "thunk" that meant we'd hit buried treasure. The children were delighted at our interest in finding bottles and joined us in our "game." Their parents were encouraging, as well, and suggested places where we could look.

A few of the islanders brought out bottles they had previously unearthed and offered to sell them for fifty cents each. There were takers— and both sides thought they got the best of the deal.

By the time we gathered our baskets and hiked back toward Sir Pat, our group had amassed thirty one old bottles altogether. Had we found none however, the day still would have been a roaring success. We needed a diversion from the sameness of the days in Victoria, and we had a wonderful adventure.

The Color of Enchantment

We sat on the plane, flying in a holding pattern for over an hour. Every once in a while, a hole in the clouds opened up and we were teased by a glimpse of the exotic land below. We knew the grand, shadowy-blue mountains were there, creating the bowl-like depression where an Indian village had become a Spanish Colonial center and then developed into a surprisingly modern city.

But the first glimpses we got were of the small fields tacked to the sides of those mountains, looking every bit like rumpled, colorful patchwork quilts thrown down by a careless hand. What we saw was magnificent and we were eager and excited about arriving in Quito, Ecuador, our second overseas post.

At last the cloud cover gave way and we floated in to a landing at the airport. We were met by colleagues from Dan's new office. Loaded into a van, we began the drive through town to the small hotel where we would be staying.

What a delight! We had never been anywhere so brazenly colorful as this place. Barefoot Indians were everywhere, most of them carrying some kind of bundle. Bags of wool, live chickens, twigs, and babies all rode securely on the backs of men, women, even children. Nearly all of them wore hats, some of them three or four at once.

But the colors! The vivid colors! Magenta, orange, green, turquoise, marigold, pure purple. When we were kids, we used to impatiently struggle to dye our Easter eggs in these shades. We never approached such perfection. The colors were in their clothing, on the cars and buses, and reflecting back at us from sky, trees and flowers.

During our first couple of days in town we made some acquaintances, Dan through work related introductions and I at the hotel where a few other new families were staying. One such family, who arrived the week before we did, had nine children.

For the life of me, I couldn't imagine traveling the world, moving every two or three years, with nine children! They recently had been in Paris and I asked the mother how they managed to keep track of everyone as they passed through busy airports. "Easy," she said. "We dress all of them alike. Everybody. In blue jeans and bright, identical t-shirts. If anyone strays, every person in the terminal knows where he or she belongs." We confess to copying their idea a couple of times. It did make it easier to keep our three children herded together.

On our third day in Quito, Dan learned that he needed to fly to Guayaquil on the Pacific coast the next morning, to check in at the office there. By the time he joined us in the hotel that evening and packed an overnight bag, both little boys were fussy. Penn, then two years old, and Sam, ten months, had colds and were slightly feverish. As most parents would react to the situation, we weren't overly concerned, but kept an eye on them.

The next morning, Dan gave each of us a kiss, then left for the airport, saying, "See you tomorrow afternoon."

He had been gone about an hour when I realized that Sam was unusually lethargic and his temperature had risen significantly. As I prepared to give him a bottle of juice, his little body stiffened and he had a seizure.

It didn't last long, but I was terrified. New to the city, alone and knowing almost no one, I didn't even know a doctor to call. Fortunately, Dan had left the telephone number for the embassy. I dialed it and the helpful lady working the switchboard was able to give me a number for an embassy-recommended pediatrician.

I called Dr. Espinosa and described Sam's condition. His order: "Bring the baby to the hospital immediately. I'll meet you there." Hurrying downstairs, I left Penn with another young CIA wife who had recently arrived. I had met Judy only once, but trusted Penn to her care for the time being.

In the hotel office, I asked the manager to call a taxi. He wrote the addresses for both the hospital and hotel on a paper so I could simply point out my desired destination to the taxi driver. I was too worried to even try to communicate in Spanish at that moment, not that anyone would have been able to understand me, anyway.

At the hospital, Dr. Espinosa examined Sam, and then admitted him. He wanted the baby kept under observation until at least the next day. I stayed with little Sam for a couple of hours, then, when he fell asleep, returned to the hotel to collect Penn from Judy.

Penn was napping on the sofa in Judy's living room when I got there. Waking him, and noting a continuing fever, I sat him up. He looked at me— and vomited halfway across the room. Now what?

Judy, tall and slender, with dark cloudy curls, had become kind and concerned new friend and she waved us out to the stairway, urging me to telephone the doctor again, this time about Penn. Back in our rooms, I made the call and the doctor repeated previous instructions: "Bring him to the hospital immediately. I will meet you there." This was turning into a bit of a nightmare.

Recognizing that we needed some serious assistance, I then called Dan's office. Managing to reach the chief of station, I explained our developing crisis. Was there any way Dan could be notified? The chief said, "Hold on. Stay where you are. We'll be right there."

Unknown to me at the time, that telephone call set a chain of helpful activity into motion, with a whole group of station and embassy people eventually stepping in to support us. The office contacted Dan, but because the airport was closed due to fog, it was another day before he was able to return to Quito.

Both boys were diagnosed as having meningitis, although of different kinds. Sam suffered from viral meningitis, the less serious variety. Penn, on the other hand, had been stricken by bacterial meningitis, the highly contagious, often fatal disease. We were told he might not survive.

In the first few days, when Penn was in very grave condition, the chief's wife Posey somehow managed to locate three English speaking private nurses who rotated eight-hour shifts in caring for a little boy who understood no Spanish. After four days, when Sam was released from the hospital, Posey and her husband took the baby to their house nearby. Meanwhile, one of the secretaries went to the hotel and took our cat to her house to free us from its care.

After a little over a week, as Penn slowly began his recovery and was removed from isolation, another wife, Pat, pitched in. She organized a schedule that saw a different mom come in every afternoon for the next two weeks to sit with Penn. These lovely, caring women brought books, records, puppets and little cars to help entertain him, leaving me free to get away for a few hours to spend some time with Sam.

We thought we were alone in a new, strange country. It turned out that people were willing to rally around us, to become substitute family. They did so much and we were so full of gratitude, we asked, "How can we ever thank you? How can we repay your kindnesses?"

Pat had the perfect answer. "We're in this together," she said. "As you travel beyond Quito, look for ways to help others. If you do that, you will be returning any favor you received here." We have never forgotten.

After Penn recovered, we left the hotel and moved into our house, settling into a wonderful stay in Ecuador. We discovered beautiful lakes and rivers where we could fish and picnic. We visited the equatorial monument just outside Quito and learned that, due to a surveyor's error, the monument is seven miles off line. Then we located the marker for the true equator running diagonally across the road in an area well off the beaten tourist path. And we searched out as many Indian markets as we could find. We still were captivated by the colors of the country.

We also were enchanted by the exotic nature of the city of Quito. It is a wonderful blend of very old and very new. In the old section of town, the narrow cobblestone streets run between rows of tall homes, whitewashed so often that the layers of paint have added a plumpness to their years. Most of them have balconies buttressed by railings of carved wood or graceful wrought iron and, by law, all the woodwork is painted blue. In the area around the old colonial government palace, one immediately sees a strong Spanish influence in the architecture.

As the city has grown, the new neighborhoods have expanded far beyond the old central core and houses in many of these sections showcase surprisingly modern architectural innovation and flair. Here the streets are broad and there is a familiar feel to the way churches and businesses are sprinkled among the clusters of homes.

Over time the neighborhoods have grown up the sides of the bowl that gives shape to the city and during our nearly three-year stay there, we never tired of driving up into those areas at night to look out over the lights that shimmered with an unusual clarity and brightness in the pristine Andean atmosphere.

The little boys looked forward to the daily walks we took. We plopped Sam into the stroller and away we'd go, exploring our new neighborhood. Not far away stood a large, attractive hotel. In a huge enclosure on the grounds lived a large, old Galapagos turtle. Sometimes Penn got to take a ride around the yard on its back.

Most days our route took us by a pleasant looking nursery school. Penn always was eager to stand at the fence, watching the children play. He had few playmates and recently had invented two new friends, Jim and Cathy, who quickly became the mischief-makers in our house. Maybe it was time to expand his horizons. We added his name to the waiting list at the nursery school, for him to be admitted after his third birthday.

Penn thrived at Saint Nickolas School. During his daily three-hour morning sessions, in the English-Spanish bilingual environment, his vocabulary expanded daily. He *loved* going to school. But sometimes accidents just happen.

A group of little people was playing in the wooden dugout canoe that sat in the school's yard. They were standing in a line, taking an imaginary trip across make-believe water. One of the children in the back fell against anther just in front. They all went down, like a row of living dominos.

Penn's face hit the piece of metal that originally held the oarlock. The blow broke the bone just below his nose, above his teeth. Surprisingly, a pediatric dentist had recently arrived in Quito from San Francisco and set up practice and he provided excellent care for Penn.

Later, a group of little ones was playing "zoo." Their cage was the space under a heavy oak table. Coincidentally, they all rose up together, roaring in unison. Their heads hit the top of the table at the same time. As Penn dropped back down, with front "paws" on the floor, half of the tabletop fell directly onto one hand. Most of the bones were broken and muscles and nerves were damaged.

Again we were unbelievably fortunate to find first quality medical care in this small Andean city. The specialist who cared for him routinely spent part of his year as a professor of orthopedic medicine at Harvard Medical School. Thinking about it, we were convinced that we would have been hard pressed to come up with such excellent doctors and treatment for Penn's various crises had we been living in the States.

We loved our first home in Ecuador but it had one significant problem: it was wet. All walls were plaster-covered brick. As the house was being built, the workers soaked the bricks in water before stacking and fixing them in place with mortar. As soon as walls were raised and cement ceilings poured, wet plaster was applied. No time was allowed for drying to take place.

It always felt damp inside, but at first we attributed that to its being the rainy season. Later, though, big blisters appeared on a wall in the dining room. One by one, the blisters popped, spewing grainy bits of plaster across the room. It looked like the wall had a bad case of chicken pox. And upstairs, water started running down bedroom walls and puddling on the floors.

When Penn was being treated for the meningitis, he was given massive doses of penicillin. While the medicine saved his life, it left him with a sensitivity to the drug. The house gradually developed pockets of mold and mildew and Penn responded with increasingly troublesome allergic reactions.

Finally we realized that our only option was to move to another, dryer house. Before the move could be accomplished, however, Penn developed a series of ear infections accompanied by awful earaches.

One night the little guy was miserable, crying with the pain in his ear. We called Dr. Espinosa in hopes of being able to do something to relieve Penn's distress. The doctor prescribed some fast-acting suppositories and Dan went to the pharmacy to pick them up.

Interestingly, while waiting for the medicine at the drug store, Dan was approached by another customer. The fellow appeared to simply want to chat as they waited. The man, it turned out, was a general in the Ecuadorian Air Force. Upon learning that Dan was a U.S. government official, the officer couldn't contain himself. He confided to Dan that "a very special cargo" was to be flown out of Quito that night, in just a couple of hours, in fact.

Dan was understandably puzzled. Flights *never* left Quito after about four o'clock in the afternoon. With towering mountains surrounding the city, late takeoffs were judged too dangerous. Yet, the general was suggesting a ten o'clock flight. Hmmm.

Then the general really surprised Dan. He invited him to fly along— as an observer. The destination was Panama, where the "cargo" would be unloaded. As an observer, Dan could testify to the reasonable and safe treatment of the "cargo." Fascinated, Dan deduced that an unexpected change of power in the Ecuadorian government was about to take place.

There was *no way* Dan wanted to be present for such a development. The State Department— not to mention the CIA—didn't need the kind of trouble that could escape from that sort of Pandora's box. Besides, he had to get the medicine home for Penn. So, he thanked the general for his kind invitation and departed.

Back at the house, Dan climbed the stairs and called to me, "Hey, Honey, do you want to put this suppository in Penn's ear or should I?" Ear, rear, whatever … Dan was ready to pitch in and be helpful.

"Wait! Dan, wait! I'll do it! And it *doesn't* go in his ear!" I replied.

"Oh. I thought he had an earache."

As to the late night flight with its special cargo, shortly after ten o'clock, we heard a plane take off, circle the city, then head off to the north. In the morning, we learned that the president of the country had been removed in a bloodless, non-violent coup d'etat. A military general had taken his place.

◄○►

We were fortunate to have pleasant and attractive homes at each of our posts. Our first house in Quito was particularly dramatic, built on the very edge of a deep ravine. Beyond the fence at the back of the yard the ground fell away, thirty feet down to a small dirt road. On the far side of the road, it dropped again, plunging eight hundred feet to the valley floor below.

Directly opposite the house, across the ravine, was the steep face of a mountain. It was covered with a patchwork of small fields cultivated by descendants of ancient Incans. To the left of those fields, the mountain ended abruptly, as though purposely cut away to reveal the wonderful vista. It was a beautiful expanse of land, tinted in the soft blues, greens and golds of native vegetation. And there in the distance, sitting squarely in the middle of the scene, was the classically shaped, snow-covered cone of a volcano.

On clear days, which we enjoyed most of the time, the view was magnificent. Sometimes clouds scudded along the length of the valley and we looked down on them as they dissipated, formed again and then rose to touch the flowers in our garden before floating away.

The owner of our house was also its architect. When he designed it, he took advantage of the fabulous site. Most of the exterior walls facing the vista were huge glass windows.

The entryway was striking. It was a large area, perhaps twenty feet by twenty feet, and the floor was made of big slabs of cut fieldstone. Its openness allowed those entering the house to see a panorama through the windows of the living room, dining room and study.

In one corner of the entryway was an indoor garden. Skylights were built into the ceiling above and a drain was located in the midst of plants in the center of the plot. Full of fresh greenery, the small space added a lovely touch.

As there was no central heating system in the house, we depended on fires in the oversized fireplace in the living room to take the edge off the chill in the evening air. Built for heat rather than for atmosphere, the daily fires required significant amounts of firewood. So we subscribed to a regular delivery of cords of cut eucalyptus.

The oily, aromatic wood burned with a hot, bright blaze and introduced a welcoming warmth to our living room. It also introduced scorpions to the house.

The nasty little arachnids found the pieces of wood to their liking and hid in cracks and crevices as well as under blisters in the peeling bark. When we carried firewood into the house and stacked it in the baskets on the wide hearth, the scorpions rode along. They also came calling through the drain in the floor of the indoor garden.

Generally speaking, those scorpions were dangerous but not deadly, at least to adults. If one of us were to be stung, it would be painful but, chances are, it wouldn't cause a life-threatening situation. For children, however, it could be a completely different story. So, during our occupancy of the house we were constantly on the lookout for the venomous critters.

It was while we lived in that house that little Sam began to talk. After the usual "Dada," "Mama," "more," and "NO," his first interesting word was "spidey."

He was always alert to things going on around him, more naturally observant than anyone else in the family. When he was about eighteen months old he spotted a beautiful moth, about the size of both his hands together, sunning itself on the side of the house. He stood there for the longest time, sometimes leaning close, but never touching. He was checking out every detail of the fascinating insect.

Through a window, I saw him examining the moth. Since he wasn't into any mischief, I went about whatever it was I was doing. Soon, though, his piercing screams caught my attention. I rushed out the door in time to see him running across the yard as fast as his little legs would take him, howling and flapping his arms. Alarmed, I hurried to pick him up. "What's wrong, sweetie?" I asked.

"My moff. Dat birt take my moff!" he sobbed. Sure enough, on the fence sat a bird with the moth clutched in its beak.

When it came to scorpions, Sam was as good as any First-Alert system we could have desired. And teamed up with our Siamese cat, Khli, the two of them were unbeatable. Locating a scorpion, Khli "scorped" her tail, twitching it in angry spikes over her back. Taking notice of her signal, Sam hurried to Dan or me, yelling "Spidey! Spidey!" Then he ran back to stand beside the cat. There they remained, dependable pointers, until we arrived to remove the dangerous pest.

◄○►

Just as Penn, Sam and Kinley couldn't have more different personalities, their arrival in our lives covered a wide scope, too. A friend of ours produced her four boys in a fascinating assortment of settings: the first in a garden, one on a golf course, another in a hotel and only one in a hospital. We couldn't match that particular variety— not that we wanted to— but there were some interesting contrasts, nonetheless.

Each of the kids claims a different country as a birthplace. Penn arrived in a fairly large, modern suburban medical center in Maryland. Sam was born in a very small private clinic in Curuba and Kinley joined us in a medium sized hospital run by American missionaries in Ecuador.

Penn was put in a nursery full of newcomers. Eight tiny ones were born that morning and they joined a dozen others already in residence. Two little boys were Sam's roommates, one Chinese and the other of African descent. Kinley shared the nursery in Quito with another American, the new son of a couple who were in the country working on an oil pipeline project.

Penn's arrival took many hours, in an environment that was both physically and emotionally sterile. Kinley's appearance, on the other hand, was a completely different story. Two weeks after the presumed due date, the doctor finally said, "Come in on Saturday and we'll induce labor, if the baby hasn't come by then."

So on Saturday we walked into the hospital and signed in. Just then, labor started naturally. We hurried upstairs.

Wanting to be present for the birth, Dan sat in the hallway, just outside the door of the delivery room, waiting to be summoned. He opened that week's international issue of *Time* magazine and began reading. Within minutes our friend Marg, the nurse, appeared at his side. A friendly Canadian girl, she had helped Penn through his crisis with meningitis.

"You have a little girl. There wasn't time to call you, but we'll let you see her in a few minutes," Marg grinned at Dan.

Now, that was the way to go. Half an hour, start to finish, and in a warm and friendly atmosphere.

◄○►

Sam's first memory dates from a special day when we were living in that Andean capital city. He told us about it at dinner one night, years later, when he was fifteen. As was usual at our dinner table, we were having a spirited conversation, talking about memories, funny things, exciting time, special moments. Out of the blue— he had never mentioned it before— Sam said to us, "I remember the day you brought Kinley home from the hospital after she was born."

"Oh, Sam, you can't possibly remember that," we replied in our usual supportive manner.

"But I *do* remember it," he insisted. "I was sitting at the dining room table eating cereal when the door opened and you walked in. You were carrying a baby wrapped in a blanket and I got off the chair and ran to the door so I could see her. Then you told me to go sit on the sofa, and I ran into the living room, and you came and put Kinley on my lap and I got to hold her!"

Sam was absolutely right. He even remembered the kind of cereal he was eating and described the picture on the box. He was correct, we knew, since that was the only American cereal available to us at the time.

We were amazed that Sam recalled the details of meeting his sister for the very first time. He was barely beyond babyhood himself, only eighteen months old.

When we brought the sweet tiny girl home that day, our family was complete. And the boys were at the wonderful stage when every day was full of fun and learning. Penn had recently turned three and was teaching Sam everything he knew. They ran and kicked balls and jumped off the retaining walls in our yard. They sang songs and looked at books. And they wore things on their heads. Hats, caps, helmets, old wigs and kitchen pans with handles pointed backwards. It didn't matter. They just loved wearing things on their heads.

Those were years when the kids were turning into interesting little people and developing their own definite personalities. Penn was born with a rigid view of life. He liked things to be orderly and precise. Once, when he was four, he cried when his socks didn't match his button-down shirt. Sam, on the other hand, put his t-shirts on backwards, tried to wear his shoes on the wrong feet and usually forgot to zip his pants.

Penn also liked things "official." A favorite game was putting stuffed animals in little chairs, lining them up and then pretending he was the traffic cop. He wore Mom's old white gloves and blew a whistle to control the stopping and going. He told us he wanted to grow up to be the ambassador. Then he could ride around in a big black car every day and drink beer with the generals. And what did Sam want to be when he grew up? One of Santa's elves, of course.

When Penn went off to kindergarten at the international school, he rode the school bus and carried his little lunch box. Everything was regulated and structured. He was secure and content in the routine that controlled his days. Then he carried home a note from the teacher. All was well, except that Penn needed help learning how to relax and go with the flow. On the school bus, he had elected himself "monitor." The children were supposed to stay seated and talk quietly but, in fact, they were jumping around and yelling. They weren't *following the rules*! It drove Penn crazy! He scolded the scoundrels which, of course, added to the uproar.

We tried to help Penn understand that not everyone is going to walk the same straight line he follows. Sometimes they weave back and forth across the line, but that doesn't make them really bad. It isn't the end of the world. He just had to learn to live with it. After all, he was living with Sam.

Didn't he remember how we survived the period when Sam was into the excitement of "flushing?" Even though he wasn't supposed to, Sam persisted in his game. A whole collection of matchbox cars and a fleet of little plastic boats disappeared one by one. Sam dropped them into the bowl and then a huge storm erupted and they whirled around and around and finally, to the accompanying screams of terrified passengers, were swept away, never to be seen again.

We had two bathrooms upstairs and another downstairs and eventually we would hear his progress as he made his rounds ... up the stairs, pitter-pat-pat, FLUSH ... down the hall ... pat-pat-pat, FLUSH ... As he came down the stairs toward the next bathroom, we intercepted him. One sure way to divert his attention was to point out a bug. He was happy to spend the rest of the morning watching it go about its busy insect business.

So, Penn listened to what we said. He stopped trying to direct perfect behavior among his little pals. The next thing we knew, we got another note, telling us that Penn was jumping around and yelling on the school bus.

◄○►

Dan's parents and twin brother and sister came to visit us in Ecuador and we spent the first week going from one colorful Indian market to another. Constant running around at that altitude was beginning to take its toll. One morning they were a little slower than usual in getting up and around. Before we had time to make definite plans for the day, Dan called from the office. "Better just hang around the house today," he said. "There's been a coup d'e-tat. Everything looks calm enough, but don't take any chances."

It turned out to be the kind of relaxing break we all needed. Grandad took a long nap and the teenage twins lay in the sun, working on their spring-break tans. Gramma, meanwhile, got busy with her post cards to friends back home. Sitting back with a glass of iced tea, she was thrilled to be able to write, "Having a wonderful time. We're in the middle of a real South American coup!"

It was during their visit that Sam, not yet two years old, made what we consider to be his first joke. Preparing to leave the house to do some sightseeing, Gramma patted the seat beside her on the sofa and said, "Come over here, Sam. Let's put on your shoes."

Sam approached Gramma, picked up a shoe and looked her in the eye. "No," he said. "Zapatos."

They ran through their conversation again. "Here, let's put on your shoes," said Gramma.

Sam handed the shoe to Gramma, but again replied, "No. Zapatos."

Gramma began to get the idea. Sam was telling her that in Ecuador shoes are called zapatos. So, gamely, Gramma tried once more. "Okay. Sit up here and we'll put on your 'sabatas'."

Sam ducked his head, grinned up at her and answered, "No, Gramma. Are *shoes*."

◄○►

As with all children, Penn and Sam went through the garble stage as they learned to speak. For some reason, the words "windshield wipers" illustrated real differences in their developing personalities. Penn, the all-business kid, called them "winchers." As his turn came to refer to such things, Sam, the whimsical one, dubbed them "wimpie-wipies."

Together they came up with "Shut up the beach."

One day we were driving through downtown Quito on our way to pick up Dad from work. We passed a local fat-bodied bus pulled up to the curb to load passengers. As was usual, it was a colorful sight. Bright blue paint job, decorated with red and white geometric designs. Crates of live chickens were loaded on the roof among bags and boxes. And arms and heads stuck out the open windows.

Drivers of these buses were notorious for their lack of traffic etiquette. They weren't bound by painted traffic lanes, often crowding other vehicles out of their way. They frequently bumped up and over curbs, onto sidewalks, to go around slower traffic. Cutting in front of oncoming cars in dangerous maneuvers was a particular specialty. Two buses together were a real adventure because that opened up the possibility for an urban drag race.

On that day, however, the bus we passed was simply there, doing nothing. Two little brothers in the back seat of the car spotted it, though. Pointing a finger, one called out "Shut up the beach!" which was enough to send them both into delighted shrieks of laughter.

This continued for several weeks. Whenever the boys caught sight of one of the buses, their strange cheer erupted from the back seat and they exploded in glee at their own wonderful wit. Meanwhile, we had no idea what it meant or why it caused so much delight.

The mystery was solved one dark night as we drove home after a visit to some friends. Traveling through a neighborhood without streetlights, we encountered an unfortunate and fairly common road hazard: a manhole with its cover removed. It appeared in front of us so quickly there was no time for Dan to avoid hitting it.

63

Thump! Jolt! His expletive was immediate. "Son of a bitch!"

From the back seat, Penn and Sam screamed in delicious joy. They clutched at each other, laughing so hard they could hardly breathe. Then it came: "Say it again, Dad! Say 'Shut up the beach!'"

◄○►

Our maid was named Maria and she was quite remarkable. An intelligent and ambitious Indian girl, her parents were the sort of industrious Indians we saw around the city every day. Her father wore a navy blue wool poncho and white pants that ended just below his knees. A solitary braid of shiny black hair hung down his back from under a black felt hat. Her mother was short and round and was clad in an ankle length red skirt and striped shawl that might have doubled as Joseph's coat of many colors.

In a society where Indians ranked almost as non-citizens, Maria meant to rise above her humble beginnings and to be a success. We "inherited" her from a departing embassy family who funded the classes she took in night school. Maria studied English and, by the time we hired her, she was nearly fluent.

What a help she was! She eased our way into our first Spanish-speaking post. During the day she helped with housework, patiently encouraged Penn, Sam and eventually Kinley to learn their first, basic Spanish vocabularies, and taught me how to fix ceviche, empanadas and other Ecuadorian dishes. In the evenings, she returned to school, now adding history and math to her schedule.

Not long before we were due to leave Quito, the family for whom she previously worked was transferred to Berlin, Germany. They wrote to Maria, asking if she would join them there. What an opportunity! So, as we departed to our next assignment, that special Indian girl went to Europe. While there she met and married a young Peruvian who was studying finance at a German university. Eventually they settled in Quito where he heads an accounting firm and she raises their three boys in a modern new home, with household help of her own.

Our gardener was an old Indian man, Manuel. Although he was still handsome and vigorous, we figure he was about ninety years old. He had to be. One day he came to the house accompanied by another old man who certainly was in his seventies. Manuel introduced his companion as his son.

As a gardener, Manuel provided only the basics. He mowed the grass, often with Penn pushing a little plastic mower at his side, and he planted daisies and poinsettias, which he tended with patient care. The other job he did was stripping and waxing our wooden parquet floors.

Manuel tied pads of steel wool to the bottoms of his sandals and shuffled and scuffed his way around the room. When satisfied that the old wax was gone, he swept up the dust. Then he tied heavy cloth to his feet. Applying wax to the fabric, he skated in slow motion across the floor. Finally, when the wax was dry, he replaced the cloth with pieces of soft sheepskin and, with a broom for a partner, slowly danced over the wood until it shone.

◄o►

A tall man, broad and sturdy without looking fat, and whose mild gray eyes hid a brain like a computer, Vince was one of Dan's colleagues who earlier served in a Latin American country beset by strife between the government and rebels who more or less controlled the countryside beyond the capital city. One day he left the station, accompanied by two local men, on his way to a village in the foothills of nearby mountains. They planned to talk to a group of peasants to learn about the influence the rebels seemed to be gaining over the affairs in the region.

Violence against the peasants was on the increase and recently the rebels had returned to their earlier practice of seizing any foreigners who ventured into their territory. Not long before, two Europeans touring another outlying area were murdered and their bodies dumped in front of a government building in the city center.

As Vince and his two companions drove along a rural road toward the village, they suddenly came upon a roadblock manned by members of the rebel militia. Forced to exit their vehicle with hands above their heads, they were escorted by an armed guard down a nearby pathway through the trees, as another rebel got in their car and drove it away.

In a clearing among the trees, where other rebels were gathered, the three were searched for identification and Vince's diplomatic card was seized with triumph. More correctly than they actually knew, the rebels declared him to be a "Yanqui spy" and announced that he would be executed. After conferring among themselves, they ordered Vince's companions to carry word of the death sentence back to embassy officials. They wanted the North Americans to recognize rebel strength and control.

The last thing Vince saw before he was blindfolded was the two men being led toward the road, where they would begin their long walk back to the city. Hands and feet tied with ropes, he was shoved to his knees to await the arrival of the commanding officer of the band of rebels.

Thinking furiously, Vince tried to come up with some idea of how to save his own life. A bluff seemed to be his only hope. After a couple of hours, an officer called Capitan Humberto arrived and he, too, announced that the Yanqui spy would be executed. At that, Vince launched his pitch.

Having remembered the name of the leader of the entire rebel movement within the country, as well as background information on him contained in an Agency file, Vince said, "I am a diplomat, not a spy. And I am a personal friend of Commandante Carlos Velasquez de Manzas. We attended university together in California. If you kill me, he will have your heads."

The rebels considered this statement by their captive, then asked for further details about the "friendship," perhaps as a means of testing Vince's truthfulness. With intense concentration, Vince dredged up every detail he could recall about Commandante Carlos, weaving imaginary references to his association with the rebel leader into his account. Incredibly, his bluff worked—at least for the moment.

Capitan Humberto decided to postpone the execution until he checked Vince's story with Commandante Carlos. A note was written to the leader and set off immediately with a rebel courier. Then Vince was driven to a small stone building, possibly used as a shepherd's hut in more peaceful times, in the middle of grassy fields near the sloping mountainsides. Blindfolds and ropes were removed before he was shoved into the tiny structure, and then the heavy wooden door was locked. At least he had bought himself some time. Maybe he could figure out a way to escape.

Vince was held overnight but guards sat against the only door the entire time. There was no possibility of getting away.

Meanwhile, Vince's companions had made their way back to town carrying news of his plight. The office was galvanized, with co-workers trying to come up with a plan to save him. But since the rebels surely had left the area where the capture took place and with no indication of where he currently might be held, the outcome appeared bleak.

Late the next morning, Vince was taken from his dingy little prison, again bound and blindfolded, and returned to the presence of Capitan Humberto. A response had come from Commandante Carlos. Vince fully expected to be shot immediately. However, the message from Commandante Carlos confirmed Vince's story! It verified their close "friendship" and ordered that he be released! Unbelieving, Vince struggled to keep his knees from buckling.

The rebels kept Vince with them for the remainder of that day, treating him as their guest, a friend of their leader. In the early evening, they prepared a special feast in his honor. As bizarre as the development was, Vince tried to act naturally and visit normally with his "hosts." After dark, they put him into one of their vehicles and drove him back to the city, leaving him within a half-hour walk of his office.

Relief exploding like Roman candles with every step he took, Vince hurried to the CIA station. Fellow case officers greeted him with whoops of joy and amazement, grabbing him in bear hugs and thumping him on his back. Of course, their first question was "*How* did you get away?"

Vince detailed his frantic bluff, then followed with the astonishing confirmation by Commandante Carlos that the two were close personal friends. It still was unbelievable.

In the following days, Vince and his co-workers came up with only two possible explanations for his release: either Commandante Carlos admitted to the friendship because releasing the Yanqui spy might earn him some good will with the Americans, or Carlos was confused and forgetful and actually thought Vince might have been an old college buddy. Whatever the case, Vince lived to tell his tale and we were relieved that we hadn't lost an Agency colleague and friend.

◄o►

Dan needed to visit the American Consulate in Guayaquil, so I tagged along to get a look at that Pacific port city. We were standing in the lobby of our hotel, preparing to go out for a lunch of shrimp ceviche when, suddenly, it felt as though the marble floor were being pulled out from under our feet. We lurched against each other, and then smashed into the counter. Turning, we scanned the lobby and tried to activate our mental "reset" buttons. It looked like a series of waves was rippling across the floor, making the marble undulate with an eerie fluidity.

Grabbing my arm, Dan took long strides toward the hotel entrance. Standing in the relative safety of the doorway, we could see people rush out into the street from nearby buildings. A few windows across from us broke and jagged spears of glass crashed onto the sidewalk below. And all the while, the street itself heaved in up and down swells. It looked like a humped sea serpent had found a way to swim just below the macadam surface.

Slowly it growled to a stop and was over, our first big earthquake.

Back in Quito, a few months after the shaking in Guayaquil, Dan and I decided to move our upright freezer across the room, to stand it against another wall. Somehow, two of its wheels disappeared during the previous move, so we couldn't just push and roll it. We had to tilt it from side to side and waddle it across the room. I was pregnant with Kinley at the time and midway through the job I felt really dizzy. The whole room kind of moved.

Just then a huge banging sound erupted from the kitchen. It was the heavy metal door leading out to a little courtyard in front. Who in the world could be out there, beating with such fury? Suddenly the whole room snapped back and forth. Earthquake! Whew! For a while there, I thought I was overexerting myself in my "condition."

When the shaking finally ceased, our maid Maria came down the stairs and into the room where we stood by the freezer. Her whole top half was sopping wet. She had been cleaning a bathtub when the house whipped violently. Losing her balance, she nose-dived right under the faucet where water was pouring out. Fortunately she wasn't hurt and saw the humor in her unexpected dousing.

—◦—

Once again Dan and I flew to Guayaquil, this time to pick up our car. It had just arrived in the country on a cargo ship and was awaiting us in the parking lot at the consulate. We decided to drive it to Quito ourselves rather than have it delivered since the trip would give us our first opportunity to check out our host country.

From the hot, flat coastal plain, the route we followed took us onto the gently rising shoulders of the Andes Mountains where the greenery of banana plantations stretches as far as the eye can see. Just beyond, where the road begins its climb to the top of the world, we hoped to see some of the colorful, primitive Colorado Indians who live in the jungle area.

They rubbed red clay over their skin and plastered it on their hair, making it look as though they wore tight fitting caps on their heads. They painted lines across forehead, nose and cheeks with black ashes and wore black and white striped loincloths. Bright red feathers, gathered from jungle birds, hung from their ears and decorated bands they wore around their upper arms.

Sometimes they stepped out of their primitive homes in the jungle and walked along the asphalt highway. How long would it be, we wondered, before they left their traditions behind and joined the march into the future? We wanted to see them, appreciate them, before that journey began. And we did.

Indians behind us, the last hours of the drive were dominated by a winding ascent hacked out of rock on the very edges of precipices, so steep they are nearly perpendicular. When we made our way along the road, clouds appeared above us, then below us and, at times, surrounded us completely. They were so thick we had to travel by inches, searching for a safe path along the brink of forever.

As suddenly as they descended, the clouds drifted away and we looked out over bare mountain peaks that shimmered in shades of amber, rose and delicate blue. We blinked our eyes against the pureness of the sunlight and sucked the thin oxygen deep into our lungs.

It was only a drive in the car, lasting seven or eight hours, yet it was exotic and foreign and remains a vivid memory all these years later.

Because the kids were so young, we rarely left town for more than a day while we lived in Quito but once we spent a long weekend in Panama. We stood at the Miraflores Locks and watched huge ships as they traversed the canal between Atlantic and Pacific Oceans. We rode the funny little steam driven train across the isthmus and back again, following the path of the canal. It took us on a trestle over Gatun Lake, then through thick jungle areas.

Penn stayed seated on the aisle, worried that snakes might drop out of trees and in through the open windows. He wanted no one to be in the way in case he needed to bolt to the other end of the car.

At the airport, before returning to our South American home, Dan gave both Penn and Sam five nickels to drop into slot machines. There was no age limit for those who wanted to try their luck and the boys were attracted by the blinking lights and ringing bells. They were slow and deliberate as they dropped in their coins and pulled on the handles. They wanted the fun to last as long as possible.

Sam had two nickels left in his hot little hand when he hit the jackpot and we all gaped as the money poured out. As generous as he was lucky, he saved all his winnings and then shared with the other two when we stopped at Disney World on our next home leave, which explains the two pirate guns and a stuffed Minnie Mouse doll that later took up space in the kids' toy box.

Another time we intended to spend a week at a pretty but primitive spot along the Pacific Ocean on the southern Ecuadorian coast. We stayed in a thatched roof cottage that sat under an oddly mixed stand of palm trees and pine trees. Lush tropical bushes embraced the little cottage at the edge of the white sandy beach. It was a terrific place—should have been completely restful. We left after only a few days, however.

Home beckoned when our carry-along camping stove developed a fuel leak, caught fire and nearly turned the cottage into a torch. While hurling it out the front door, Dan suffered severe burns on his hand and arm. Just about then we discovered that three-year old Sam had been spending his spare time busily stuffing bright red berries into his ears so we decided it was time to get back and check in with the doctor.

◄◦►

Cuenca is a small Andean city about two hundred miles south of Quito. It's an old, pretty Spanish Colonial town located in the mountains in the narrow handle of land between Peru and the Pacific Ocean. Industrious Indians make their way through the streets, carrying baskets overflowing with colorful flowers and bundles of beans and yarn on their way to the markets.

We were spending a long weekend there, enjoying the opportunity to see more of our host country. We wandered through the city center, admiring the architecture of the homes and the intricate wrought iron grillwork that adorned the balconies. We rested weary feet in a small plaza where the marble benches and tile walkways, even the flower beds and trees, are arranged to complement the delicate beauty of a water fountain, set in the middle of it all.

A block away from the plaza we discovered perhaps the most amazing feature of the city. Their cathedral is huge, far larger than anything we could have expected to find there. The whole area around the altar is covered in gold leaf, as are the stone garlands that twine around the columns standing in two rows down the length of the sanctuary. We expect to see magnificent churches like this throughout Europe and in very large cities in other parts of the world. But to find such a wonderful place of worship in this small, secluded town was surprising.

We were told that the cathedral was designed in Spain. Much of the building material was shipped from Europe, with other supplies gathered in other parts of South America. All of it was collected together at a single depository along the coast.

It was then carried piece by piece— huge stone blocks, tiles, pieces of columns, immense doors and the gold for decoration— on the backs of Indians, up and over the Andes mountains, before finally being assembled in Cuenca. Interesting to contemplate that such sophisticated activity was going on in that remote location as settlers were establishing tiny, crude outposts in what later would become Massachusetts, Virginia and New York.

After admiring the cathedral, we made our way to one of the nearby Indian markets where we encountered ongoing chaos. There were several hundred people taking part in market activity that day but the high spirits, energy and movement were such that the term "bustling" hardly does justice to the atmosphere we encountered.

Hemp ropes, baskets and pottery were displayed on the ground next to brightly colored blankets covered with straw ornaments, hats and paper maché masks. There were boxes and baskets full of seeds and grain. Pairs of sandals made from expired rubber tires, treads still visible on the soles, sat in rows on tables. We joined shoppers who sorted through clothing hanging from racks and admired a rainbow of ponchos available in twenty different colors, as well as hand-embroidered blouses common to the area.

As we wandered through the sea of activity we came to their equivalent of an American shopping mall's "food court." Stews in big iron kettles bubbled over beds of charcoal. We saw rows of fried pork rinds stacked next to halves of melons, a dozen varieties of bananas and unfamiliar tubers.

In the midst of it all, Indians were roasting pigs on spits over glowing embers and displaying them on trays lined with chunks of cooked plantains and potatoes. Hungry customers lined up, holding out their own tin plates and bowls, to be filled with whatever caught their fancy for that day's lunch.

We gave all of it a pass since we had plans for a mid-afternoon meal at a small hotel in a nearby town. The hotel was picturesque and appealing. Long and low, it sat on a broad gentle slope in the bend of a clear mountain river. A wide wooden porch ran along the front of the building and at one end half a dozen tables were set out for diners.

We were with our friends, Jack and Judy, another couple from the station, and after studying the menu, our unanimous dinner choice was fresh trout. It took a while to be served, but we were comfortable and content, happy to sit and visit. Finally, the platters of beautiful fish were placed in front of us. They were so large their heads and tails lopped over the ends of the oversize oblong plates.

The waiter wanted to know, "Did you see us?"

"Uhh, no. See you ... what?" we asked.

And he explained. He and another kitchen worker went down to the river after we placed our orders and they caught the trout then and there. Talk about fresh! This was Dan's kind of place! He loves to fish and in Ecuador he found more wonderful spots to enjoy that pastime than in any other country.

He fished most often at Lake Papallacta, a small mountain lake less than two hours east of Quito. Reached by traveling on a twisting dirt road that climbed over the continental divide, it lay at 12,000 feet. Because it was so near Quito, it made an easy day trip and sometimes the kids and I accompanied him.

One day we scrambled down the hill from the road and began to make our way along the edge of the lake. Dan led the way. As usual, he was serious about the business at hand and didn't mind that the kids and I dawdled. It put some distance between playtime and honest fishing.

Penn and Sam had little toy fishing poles with red and yellow handgrips. Two-inch long silver plastic fish dangled from the ends of the strings and the boys had fun swishing them through the water. Little Kinley had a tiny blanket tied around her shoulders, like a good Ecuadorian mama, and riding securely inside the bundle was her doll, Juanita.

So, Dad fished, the boys threw rocks and made splashes, Kinley picked a miniature bouquet of miniature wild flowers and I strolled along, happy with the world. As we rounded the end of the lake, Dan was well ahead of us, casting, reeling in, completely absorbed in his activity. Just then a snort made me look over my shoulder.

Behind and slightly above us, in a field strewn with large boulders, was a herd of about a dozen wild horses. The ones in front pawed the ground and jerked their heads up and down. The kids noticed them, too, and as we stood there looking, two came charging at us. About ten yards from the water they broke away and galloped back to the group. We must have been in their usual pathway to the lake. They certainly were letting us know that we were the trespassers.

Naturally, the kids were alarmed and they came running to my side. Kinley climbed up into my arms and the boys grabbed my legs as the horses charged again, then veered away as before. I took three-year-old Sam by the hand and spoke quietly to Penn, "Don't scream and cry. Don't let them know we're afraid. Let's be very brave and back away from the horses. Okay?"

As brave as any four year old could be, Penn rose to the challenge. He plastered a sickly grin on his frightened little face and squeaked out a chant, "Heh-heh, heh-heh," as we retreated from the area the horses seemed to want to claim. When we were far enough away to satisfy the animals, they rushed to water's edge, then turned and raced back to wherever they came from. Meanwhile, Dan was completely oblivious to our adventure, caught up as he was in his favorite pastime.

He fished at that lake about once a month and that probably wasn't often enough from his point of view. One time he took a visitor from the States with him and they returned to the house that evening with a dozen beautiful fish, their choice of "keepers" from a total catch of over fifty trout that day. The man was so thrilled with their good luck on the outing that, as he cleaned and filleted the fish at our outdoor sink, he rhapsodized about the experience. Dan leaned against a nearby wall and let his friend talk— and work.

Sometimes Dan went with his fishing buddies to a stretch along the Rio Salido, a river that flows out of Lake Papallacta into the jungle region of the Amazon basin. There, in the primitive area, they found clear gentle water, vines and orchids hanging from rain forest trees and fat green iguanas sunning themselves on rocks along the river. And fish.

But their favorite fishing spot was Lake Micacocha, a frigid mountain lake sitting at the base of a snow capped volcano. Located above the tree line at 15,000 feet, it was a cold and miserable place to camp. Each time they made the trek to the lake, it either snowed or rained a mixture of slush and ice pellets. The lake was so remote, Dan and his friends even needed a guide to reach it.

Sam Hogan was that guide. A retired U.S. Army Colonel and former Defense Attaché at the embassy in Quito, Sam stayed on in Ecuador after his tour there, and established a sporting guide business. He was a delightful man, an outdoors Texan who graduated from West Point. He was well known to historians as the officer in charge of Task Force Hogan during the Battle of the Bulge in World War II.

Germans near the Ourthe River in Belgium surrounded his group, part of the third Armored Division, on December 21, 1944. Under Sam's command, the men of the Task Force, dubbed "Hogan's 400" by the American press, destroyed their vehicles and slipped away through enemy lines. Alternating marching and hiding from the Germans, every single one of Sam's soldiers reached the American lines by December 26.

Dan didn't learn about Sam's place in World War II history until we were ten years beyond Ecuador. While we were there, Sam talked about hunting and fishing rather than himself. Not only did he guide Dan and his friends to the lake, he also did all the organizing, even arranging for an Indian to act as "camp boy" at the lake. But it wasn't a matter of simply pampering and privilege for the Gringos.

The altitude was so extreme that those unused to being at 15,000 feet had to be careful not to over-exert themselves. Altitude sickness, caused by oxygen deprivation, can be a serious, debilitating condition. So, although they risked constant headaches, Dan's group concentrated on "sport" while the camp boy set up the tents and fixed their meals. Other Indians and their horses were on hand to pull the boats between the camp and the lake.

Listening to Dan's talk about their camping arrangement, I sometimes wondered if having servants along on a fishing trip wasn't a bit excessive. But the guys all loved going there and, to be honest, it was the fish that drew them. They were the biggest trout any of them had ever seen. Some were thirty inches long and, because of the extremely cold water, their flesh was as red as any salmon meat. Virtually any fish caught was a keeper.

We remember Dan's return from one of those outings, when he brought back nine trout totaling over fifty pounds. Some had to have heads and tails removed before they fit into our upright freezer.

◄○►

After nearly three years of enjoying the colors of Ecuador, it was time to move on. We packed up and headed back to the States for six weeks of home leave. Turned out to be the most hair-raising return trip home we ever made. We lost Kinley.

We flew into Miami. Fifteen suitcases, three kids, ages two, three and five, and assorted carry-on toys. We also had the cat and dog, in sky cages, that had to be cleared through customs and then shipped onward to Baltimore where Gramma and Grandad would pick them up.

Our good friends Dennis and Linda met us at the airport with plans to spend the night with us in the airport hotel before we flew to California the next day. They had their two young children with them so, with their family added to our mix, the swirl of activity and confusion was impressive.

In the midst of it all was tiny Kinley in her pink dress and carrying a very strange looking baby doll in matching pink. Like the rest of us, the doll was moving from Quito's 10,000-foot altitude to sea level in Florida.

When the plane landed, air pressure inside the doll's head didn't equalize immediately and its dimpled face collapsed in on itself. Her eyes, nose and mouth disappeared as the forehead bent down to meet her chin. With so much else going on as we arrived, first aid on the doll would have to wait until we got into our rooms in the hotel.

Dog and cat seen to, we finally made our way from the terminal, down a long corridor to the hotel lobby. As Dan checked us in and Dennis arranged for a porter to load the luggage onto carts, the kids of both families played hide and seek among the chairs and sofas. We were assigned to rooms on the eighth floor and, big people, little people and suitcases, we loaded into three elevators.

Meeting each other at the upper level, we proceeded around corners and down hallways. Midway to our rooms, I counted heads and came up one short. Clutching at— and practically shredding— Dan's shirt sleeve, I managed to ask in a strangled voice, "Where is Kinley?"

"I don't have her. *You* do," he answered.

"No, I don't. *Where is she?*"

Linda took the four remaining kids, plus luggage, to our adjoining rooms. Dennis started down the stairs, on his way to check outside the hotel. Dan returned to the lobby to look for her and ask for help. He talked to several people, giving descriptions of both Kinley and her doll. Then he started searching in the general area of the lobby where we remembered last seeing her.

Meanwhile, I got on an elevator, returned to the lobby, and then rode to the top of the hotel, stopping at each floor. We wondered if Kinley might have got off one of the elevators during a possible stop on our ascent. As the door opened, I stepped out, called "*Kinley!*" listened for an answering cry, and then went on to the next floor. The higher I rose in the building, the more frantic I felt.

Leaping out at the top floor, blind panic clutching my heart, I screamed, "*Kinnlleeyy!!*" Only when I really looked did I realize I was standing in the middle of a restaurant, full of startled diners. Quickly, very quickly, I stepped back into the elevator and convulsively punched the button to close the door. During the ride back down to the lobby— and occasionally over the years since then— I wondered just *what* those people thought.

There in the lobby, at that point about fifteen minutes into our worry, I met Dan who was carrying Kinley in his arms. Thank God.

A businessman, visiting the States from England, had responded to Dan's plea for help. He walked down a long hallway lined with windows featuring colorful travel advertisements. Near the end of the hallway, looking in a window full of everything blue, stood little Kinley. Noting the unique doll, he knew he'd found the missing child and the kind gentleman returned her to us.

It Wasn't Always Easy

I fell in love with the house in Santiago, Chile, our third overseas post, the moment we drove into the driveway with the real estate agent. Set on a large lot and surrounded by mature shade trees, the house was beautifully proportioned and had a gracious air that was warm and inviting. Three sets of French doors, flanked by white slatted shutters, led onto a red tile patio that ran the length of the house.

Upstairs, three other sets of French doors invited sunshine and soft breezes into the bedrooms. The rooms were spacious, with high ceilings, and a graceful curving staircase rose from the entryway to the second floor.

In the best of times it must have been a truly elegant home. Our stay there was not during the best of times, however, so we encountered a sort of dilapidated splendor. Because of the political upheaval in Chile, the owners of the property had left the country and were unwilling to invest in costly maintenance. When we signed the lease to rent the house, we became resident caretakers who had to accept the property "as is."

The one thing the landlord did agree to update was the old fashioned kitchen. It was a shambles. The few cabinets and cupboards drooped from the walls, half of their doors broken or missing, and green and brown paint flaked onto the floor. The outdated, leaky enamel sink was cracked and chipped. It stood on metal legs beneath the window, where it provided only cold water.

After we moved into the house, the entire room was remodeled and fitted with new cabinets and stainless steel sink. We were so pleased with the new kitchen, hot water included, that we accepted the dinosaur of a furnace with barely a whimper.

The kerosene-fired unit was ancient and completely inadequate for a house of that size. When it worked, it heated only the lower floor. So we dressed the kids in warm pajamas and were grateful for small blessings. Fortunately, Santiago enjoys a climate so temperate that we rarely had to fire up the old beast. But lighting the furnace occasionally had to be undertaken and the exercise was, well, primitive.

We straightened out a wire clothes hanger, leaving a small loop on one end. Winding a rag strip around the loop, we then plunged it into a kerosene-filled peanut can. Next, we pumped a priming button half a dozen times and rotated a lever, opening the valve that set the fuel flowing. At this point we had to act fast or the kerosene would begin to pool on the cement floor under the furnace, setting the stage for the possibility of future excitement.

Lying on the floor, we grabbed the coat hanger out of the peanut can and lit the fuel-soaked rag with a wooden match. At a full stretch, we guided the torch back and under the antique unit and waited for the kerosene to catch. In the cramped space, we tried to anticipate the moment of ignition.

It was almost a game, trying to roll out of the way of the cloud of black, oily soot that immediately belched forth. There was no escaping at least a light coating of soot on face and arms during the process, but agility determined just how black we were when we emerged from the furnace room.

We had to repeat the routine three or four times during the winter. Of course, by the time we were into our third cold season there, and getting adept at stoking the fire, it was time to move again. No matter. We loved living in that house.

The yard was really wonderful. It was the kind of place every child would like to have. It had a big, open lawn where the kids chased around, playing Superman with towels pinned at their necks like capes. They rode bikes and scooters down the long driveway and played cowboys and Indians in the green tunnel formed by the fence on one side and trees and bushes on the other.

Then there was the swimming pool. It was terrific! We didn't care that the paint was faded and tiles around the pool were cracked. We didn't care that the drain was so overgrown with roots that we had to pump out the final two feet of water by using a tiny make-shift pump fashioned from a lawn mower engine. We didn't even care that the water used to fill it came from snowmelt, directly off the Andes Mountains rising from the valley behind us. It was so cold that we had to wait a week before we could get in and splash around without turning blue.

What mattered was that we had that swimming pool. With our friends often joining us, we used it constantly during the southern hemisphere summers.

Before filling the pool the very first time, we enrolled the kids in swimming lessons. They were held in the pool at the ambassador's residence. Penn had just turned six, Sam was four and Kinley was two months shy of her third birthday. It was interesting to see how each approached the lessons.

Little Kinley had no fear at all. It was a game. On the first day, she mastered the doggy paddle and was leaping off the diving board the next. Penn looked at swimming lessons as a challenge and went about learning with a serious determination. Sam didn't like to get water in his face. He held back. He preferred to hunt for caterpillars in the bushes that lined the fence around the pool.

One day it was time for the four-year-old group to gather poolside. Where was Sam? Not around the pool. I checked in the bushes. Not there, either. Moving out into the grounds of the residence, I searched for him and called his name. Finally there came an answering response. Heading in that direction, I spotted him— at the very top of the tall flagpole.

While waiting near the pool, he spied the gold ball atop the pole. "That looks interesting. Forget the dumb swimming lessons," he reasoned. He slipped away and within minutes the wiry little boy shinnied twenty feet up to touch the ball.

Reluctant to yell and perhaps startle him, I gritted my teeth and said, matter of factly, "Okay, c'mon down. Your turn in the pool." So, as fast as a monkey on uppers, down he slid. Not for the first, or last, time I considered buying a leash.

During the warm months, our lives centered around the pool. We swam every day. Dan bought a small rubber boat and tossed it in and the kids were in and out of it constantly. Even the dog, funny little Charco, liked riding around in it.

Then Dan decided to put the pool to another use. It was time to teach the kids how to fish. Or, at least, how to cast. He tied old keys to the ends of their lines and stood the kids along one end of the pool. He put floating swim toys in the water and had the kids aim at specific targets. Anyone who hit the bulls-eye, or even came close, was rewarded with money!

Since Chilean escudos at the time were worth about as much as Monopoly money, the bills didn't represent a big investment. To the kids, though, folding money meant "riches." They spent happy weekend afternoons, with Dad as coach, amassing personal fortunes.

—◦—

Before moving into this happy home, we spent nearly three months living in embassy-provided temporary quarters. A typical apartment building, there were two apartments on each of the four floors and the structure filled nearly the entire lot. Only a sidewalk separated it from the street in front and another sidewalk and a small driveway ran along one side. In the back there was an area where ashes and clinkers from the central furnace were dumped. Garbage cans for the eight apartments leaned against the walls like exhausted soldiers.

The kids were little then and there was no grassy yard for them to run around in. One day, they went outside to play with little toy cars on the sidewalk next to the building. After a while, when I no longer heard their voices through the open kitchen window, I went to check on them. They had grown bored with their game and discovered the dump area out in the back.

Someone in the building had discarded several strings of raw sausages, leaving them just within the kids' reach. Oh, what a treat! Soft and squishy and a lovely shade of green, the sausages were eagerly snatched up by little hands. "What can we do with these?" they asked each other. "How can we play 'snakes'? Ah! I know! Stuffed whips!"

By the time I located them, they were well into a spirited battle. They dragged the sausages along the ground and through the clinkers, and then lashed each other over the head and across the body. Of course the grease in the sausages acted like a magnet for the ashes. Those little ones were nearly unrecognizable, covered as they were with black stripes on faces, arms and legs and globs of meat hung from their hair and clothes.

It was in that same apartment where we first encountered "califonts." Gas-fired flash heaters mounted on the wall, they heated water as it was needed. Simply turning on the tap triggered the heating action. Moving water opened a little valve, releasing gas. The pilot light lit the gas and heating began as water moved through the pipe. When the tap was turned off, water movement stopped and the gas valve closed.

We had one califont. It was in the full bathroom located at the back of the apartment. It heated water for our whole unit, including the kitchen and half bath, both located in the front of the apartment. When we wanted to wash dishes in the kitchen, we had to let the water run for a couple of minutes to give time for it to be heated by the califont and then flow through the pipes to the other end of the apartment.

If hot water didn't appear after a reasonable wait, we had to check the califont since sometimes the sudden gust of gas being released for ignition blew out the pilot light. And if the pilot light was out, we had to relight it.

To get to the califont, we stepped onto the toilet lid and then up onto a tiled half-wall built around the shower and tub. Using a wooden match, we guided the flame inside the unit, between coiled tubes.

By the time we turned off the tap in the kitchen, walked to the other end of the apartment, climbed the wall and dropped all the matches on the floor, we always forgot the fact that gas had been escaping into the air for several minutes. As soon as the match was inserted into the slot on the side of the califont ... *Whoom!* ... a noisy, yet harmless explosion occurred. Picking ourselves up off the floor, we tried again.

We weren't the only forgetful ones. Several times a week we heard, from some other apartment in the building, the familiar: WHOOM! Thud! "Damn!"

◄○►

Food was a serious matter during the early days of our stay in Santiago. Political upheaval racked the country and a truckers' strike resulted in a blockade of the city. As the months wore on, there were terrible food shortages.

Long lines snaked out doors and down the street from any shop that managed to acquire a supply of cooking oil or flour or other such staple. Rationing was a by-product of the shortages so we learned to carry along an empty bottle and a plastic bag whenever we left the house. That was in case we ran across a store doling out small portions of something, anything to customers.

Once, while traveling in an unfamiliar part of the city, we spotted a long line of people patiently waiting alongside a high brick wall. Thinking that a nearby shop must have a supply of *something* good, we parked the car, hopped out and, bottles and bags in hand, hurriedly joined the queue. After ten minutes or so, we learned we were among those waiting to visit inmates in the local prison.

To buy soft drinks and beer, we needed empty bottles to exchange for full ones. Those of us new to the country had to depend on people departing post to pass along their collection of empties to us. Dave and Ruth were another young couple who arrived about the same time we did and they lived two floors above us at the apartment house. We pooled our resources and within a month had several dozen empties between us.

It wasn't a simple matter to just run to the store to trade them in for full bottles, however. Neither couple had a car yet, and buses operated sporadically, if at all. So, every week or two, Dan and Dave loaded the bottles into the kids' little wagon and took an early evening stroll to shops in the surrounding neighborhoods.

Sometimes they were successful in their search. A few times they even found such treasures as a dozen eggs or a few boxes of noodles and they snatched them up. But just as often, their walks turned out to be nothing but walks.

Once Dan and I went out, intending only to window shop in an area filled with clothing and gift boutiques. We happened upon a small store that had received an unusually large supply of light bulbs. In that time and place, light bulbs were extremely hard to find. Who knew when we would locate them again? So, in a victorious mood, we happily purchased four dozen light bulbs and later shared them with friends.

Of greater concern to us were basic foodstuffs. Shortages really were severe. We got a loaf of bread in March, our first week in Santiago, and we didn't see another loaf until the following September. Meanwhile, the kids got used to peanut butter and jelly sandwiches made with water biscuits, two-inch disks similar to hard soda crackers. Once or twice a month our gardener was able to bring us half a dozen fresh rolls he bought at a government-subsidized bakery in his neighborhood on the other side of the city.

The blockade of the city, the cause of the food shortages, was also the reason we didn't yet have a car. Until the traffic arteries into the city were opened up, there was no way our vehicle could be delivered to us. With the public transportation system at a near standstill, it was exceedingly difficult for us to make our way around town on shopping expeditions. It was a stroke of luck, then, to meet Marisa.

Inflation was progressing in quantum leaps and everyone was feeling the pinch. Marisa's husband was a lawyer but his income was no longer enough to support their family. A serene, dark haired woman with a face like a Walt Disney princess, she was eager to find a way to earn some extra money and I needed to get out to buy groceries. It suited us both when she agreed to be my driver.

We started out by shopping one day a week, but that simply wasn't enough time. Trying to locate food became a quest. We settled on Mondays and Thursdays and we spent hours making our rounds. A pound of rice here, a jar of honey there. We couldn't find tuna but for a while there was a whole shelf of lovely canned crab in one shop. We never came across bags of granulated sugar so we eagerly snatched up a couple of boxes of hard-as-rock sugar cubes. Hey, it worked!

As inflation roared out of control, shop owners stopped putting prices on individual packages. They even ceased displaying prices on the shelves. It wasn't worth the trouble. The value of the escudo, the Chilean monetary unit at the time, was changing so rapidly that assigning values to goods could hardly keep up.

Finally, most of the shops we visited resorted to a very basic system. As there were only a few items available on the shelves, each product was listed on a chalkboard displayed at the cashier's counter. It got to the point that the prices were chalked in first thing in the morning, then erased and updated two or three times during the day.

On the open market, beef was a thing of the past. So was pork. And lamb. Sometimes we could get a chicken and occasionally some fish. However, butcher shops usually could be counted on to have a supply of one thing: horse meat.

Being a typical American, my initial reaction to buying horsemeat was *no way!!* Hunger sometimes can make a difference in one's outlook, though. Eventually I gave in and bought a chunk. With fresh vegetables still available, we had horse stew on our table that night.

I bought some more. Horse stroganoff, horse pot roast. Dan and the kids ate it. But no matter what seasonings or sauce or wine I added to disguise the flavor, it was still horsemeat. Nope. It didn't work. We returned to meals of soups and salads, supplemented by occasional chicken, fish or eggs.

Not surprisingly, the ones hurt most during this period were the middle class Chileans. The rich were able to leave the country and carry on. Adequate food was provided to the poor through government-subsidized programs in the poverty stricken "barrios" or slums on the edges of the city. The middle class was left to manage as best it could.

The whole situation in Santiago continued to deteriorate. Finally, Marisa and her family gave up the struggle and went to Argentina to stay with cousins. At just about that time, Dan and I were invited to a dinner party by a couple from the embassy.

What a dinner! Twelve of us sat down to roast beef with all the trimmings! After the meal, as sometimes happens, the group split, the men at one end of the living room, women at the other. As we began to chat, I wasted no time asking the hostess where she got the meat. She answered, "Through the black market, of course." Then she went on to gush about all the wonderful cuts of beef in her freezer. Pork and chicken, too. Hmmm.

"What is the black market? Where is it? What's available there?" I asked, excited to know that, somehow, food *was* available. The hostess and the other wives just sat there and looked at me. No one answered.

In frustration, I explained about the difficulties we were having trying to find foodstuffs, of any kind, for our family. "If food is available out there, I need to know how to get it. Won't you please help us?"

At last the hostess cleared her throat. And then, in a generous gesture, one American to another, as a supportive fellow embassy wife, she said, "I'm sorry, but I can't tell you. If too many people place orders through the black market, there might not be enough for *my* family." Aaargh! I still can't believe it!

The next afternoon our telephone rang. It was Mary, one of the wives who had attended the dinner party. "I apologize," she said. "I can't let this go on. I'll take you to the black market. When would you like to go?" Bless you, Mary.

It was a kind of warehouse. No signs on it, nothing to attract attention. Just an average looking building in a slightly rundown commercial district. But inside it was heavenly. We weren't looking for luxury goods or gourmet delights. We needed basics. And blockade-runners had gathered what we needed.

Sugar, flour, salt, powdered milk and cereal. There was coffee and tea, oil, rice and noodles. Tomato sauce, vinegar, detergent, toothpaste and toilet paper. Fresh meat and poultry. There it all was! Thrilled beyond words, I made a list and asked about prices of each item. I bought nothing that day. But I'd be back— soon.

◄○►

The value of the escudo was pegged to the U.S. dollar. Officially, one U.S. dollar would buy sixty escudos when we arrived in Santiago. Beyond the borders of the country, however, the rate was 1:500—and climbing all the time. The escudo was worth less every day.

With inflation getting totally out of hand, a monetary black market opened up. Enterprising Chileans crossed borders into Bolivia, Argentina and Paraguay, traveled to countries even further away, and bought escudos at the outside world's exchange rate. They smuggled the money back into the country and re-sold it at a slightly lower rate, but much higher than the legal rate.

Officially, the embassy had to recognize the Chilean government's exchange rate. As a practical matter for us as individuals, however, there was no reason, apart from an ingrained vestige of piety, perhaps, to endure true financial hardship by sticking to the prescribed, yet artificial, exchange rate. Eventually, virtually everyone in the embassy made use of the black market money, even though the practice never could be officially advertised or condoned.

The exchange rate kept going up. On the black market, one dollar bought 700 escudos two weeks ago. It was 1:900 last week, 1:1,200 today. Eventually it topped an unbelievable 1:2,500. The national bank printed more and more currency, in ever-larger denominations. In truth, the small bills now weren't worth the paper they were printed on.

Soon after we moved into our house, a man came to measure the windows for curtains. We settled on fabric and color. And price. We agreed that the curtains were worth $500 in U.S. dollars. We would pay the man for the curtains in escudos in two installments. Half would be paid in two weeks' time and the remainder paid when the curtains were completed two weeks after that. And we would pay at the black market rate. Otherwise, the shop would lose our order or be unable to acquire the needed fabric. You understand.

Two weeks after placing the order, I went to pay the first installment. The $250 was worth a lot of escudos on the black market that day. I carried the bills to the shop in a paper bag.

When we prepared to pay the second installment, the exchange rate had risen so high that we had to stack packages of new bills, still bound with paper strips, in a cardboard box. Obviously, the curtain maker couldn't count every bill. He started to count the packets of money, then waved it off. "I believe you," he said. "At this rate, what does it matter?"

Prices on everything rose by the day, if not by the hour. Items in demand found their way into the black market system and costs went up accordingly. As long as we used black market money to buy black market goods, we managed just fine. Had we continued to get our escudos at the official exchange rate, buying the things we really needed would have been almost impossible.

Making a few sacrifices and enduring a few hardships while serving our government was one thing. But not having enough food for our children or being unable to pay for heating fuel or electricity was something else altogether.

◄○►

I couldn't wait for Dan to get home from work that night. "Look! Look what food we can get at the black market!"

We sat down together and examined the list. Immediately, we knew we had to share access to this food with our friends at the embassy. Several couples who arrived in country around the same time we did also were having difficulties finding sufficient food. At least half a dozen singles who worked full time were hampered, as well, since they didn't have enough time to search out things they needed.

We organized the list and typed it up, making the page into an order blank. We counted those who probably would want to join in a combined order. Dan made copies of the order blank the next day in his office, and then passed them around. We allowed three days for our friends to return their orders to us.

Early the next week, all orders in hand, we combined the requests. Sixty pounds of rice, fifteen gallons of oil, ten bags of sugar, three dozen boxes of spaghetti. And so it went. Returning to the black market warehouse, I placed the huge order. All the food would be delivered to our house where our friends would pick up their orders when they could.

We had plenty of room. Just as our car couldn't reach us through the blockade, our furniture shipment was likewise delayed. We were more or less camping out in the house, using a few pieces of furniture borrowed from the embassy warehouse.

We slept on mattresses on the floor. The old sofa in the living room had legs on only one end. We put bricks under the other end and sat gingerly. A few cases of food stacked here and there against the bare walls wouldn't be a problem.

The black market merchants preferred to make the delivery after dark, to avoid unnecessary attention. About nine o'clock the truck arrived. There were so many items, it took nearly twenty minutes to unload it all.

The bags of sugar were very large, each weighing twenty kilograms. That's forty four pounds. The deliverymen stacked them in two piles, five bags high, just inside our front door.

Over the next several days our friends came and claimed their goods. Finally, what remained were the things we ordered. After stacking bottles, jars, boxes and cans of foodstuffs on the shelves in our pantry, I stood back and smiled. There's a sense of security in having a well-stocked larder, I thought. What a wonderful day! Things are really looking up!

That's when I decided to scoop the forty four pounds of sugar into individual gallon-size plastic bags, thinking it would be easier to store and use the sugar if it were in smaller quantities. What I didn't know was that when the deliveryman plopped our bag of sugar down and shoved it into place during the late-night unloading, a small tear in the heavy paper bag resulted, but went unnoticed.

When I opened the large bag, the sugar was crawling with tiny ants! Obviously, the small hole was the only invitation the ants needed. For those ants, we're talking party time!

Oh, dear. Now what? We couldn't just throw the sugar out. It was too hard to come by and, in our situation, waste was unthinkable. I tried sifting the sugar, but the ants were too tiny to be trapped by the fine mesh. Next, I began to dip the sugar out of the bag by the spoonful. But, forty four pounds!

Finally, I hit on a workable solution. Covering one end of the table with waxed paper, I spread the sugar a cup at a time. Then I dipped my finger in a glass of water and Dot! Zot! Zap! plucked the ants away from the grains of sugar. The next time I dipped my finger into the glass, the ants remained behind in the water. It took a couple of days to complete the job but the sugar was saved.

◄○►

No matter how you look at it, the first six months we spent in Chile were difficult. And that difficult time culminated in a coup d'etat so violent it qualified as a mini-war, which left us reeling for months.

The blockade of the city, resulting from the truckers' strike, caused shortages not only of food but also of fuel and other consumables. One embassy family was unable to locate repair parts for their nonfunctioning furnace on the local market. The pieces ultimately were mailed to them, through the diplomatic pouch from the States. But meanwhile, since the furnace fired their boiler, they were without both heat and hot water. Cold water showers in an already cold house just wouldn't do.

They worked out a schedule, showering sometimes at a tennis club, other times at homes of friends. We hosted them on Friday nights. After their three kids were scrubbed and in clean pajamas, they played with our kids while the mom and dad showered and shampooed. Then we played pinochle for a couple of hours before they headed home. After a few weeks, it didn't seem unusual at all.

More and more often, rioting broke out in the city. Hardly any section was spared the sight of overturned buses being burned and crowds of people running to escape clouds of tear gas. Everything was getting out of control.

Trucks full of increasingly scarce heating fuel were rarely seen on the streets any more. When they did venture out, it was at the risk of being stopped at gunpoint and forced to make a delivery at an unscheduled address. Newspaper reports of the strong-arm tactics served as "how-to" lessons and the practice spread. Even service stations tried to intercept each other's deliveries of gasoline.

At one point, a school bus full of our embassy children was stopped, then boarded by a self-proclaimed militia group. As guns were pointed at the children, the men searched the Donald Duck and Sesame Street lunch boxes. But for what?

Penn was only five years old so we decided to keep him out of the International school and to place him in a tutorial program, instead. It was based on the home study Calvert system from Baltimore. Penn and a little girl named Terri were the first two students who began meeting with the teacher in an apartment every morning.

As the situation at the International school deteriorated— no fuel for the furnace nor for the school buses, harassment of the children, closing of the school for weeks due to bureaucratic annoyance— more and more parents switched their children to the Calvert program.

It wasn't long before it became an actual small school. More teachers were hired and they moved to a large house, with spacious rooms and an enclosed courtyard where the kids could safely play. Best of all, it was located in the residential area where most of us lived, so the children were just minutes from their homes. We all felt it was safer for them there.

The strain of the situation wasn't lost on the children. One afternoon Penn sat beside me, quiet for a few minutes. Then he looked in my eyes and admitted, "I don't think I like Chile, Mom. It's just problems, problems, problems. Isn't it?" Out of the mouths of babes ….

As for Dan, like the rest of the people who worked in the embassy, he made an effort to vary his route to and from work. Any kind of definite pattern can leave a person open to an attack by terrorists. So he followed the suggestions issued by the security office, to use different streets as he drove an office carpool vehicle between home and work at different times each day. *Being alert* became second nature to him.

When he was out of the office during the day, whether for lunch or on an errand, he learned to "read" the atmosphere. Too many people or too few people on the street could spell trouble. A sort of cloudy fog a couple of blocks away almost certainly meant tear gas. It's strange now to think of how easily we slipped into casual acceptance of his reports of rioting and running as he went about his daily routine.

As the situation became more tense and stressful, a meeting of embassy wives was called. Held at the ambassador's residence, the ambassador himself came to sit with us and frankly discuss what was going on. He said that all indications pointed toward an eventual rupture of the current government, though by what means he didn't know.

He suggested that we try to stockpile food and water, in case of an extreme emergency situation. He also asked us to keep an eye on each other. If we noticed a friend beginning to crack from the pressure, we should offer what support we could.

It was an unusual meeting, to say the least. In hindsight, one wonders why the dependent wives and children weren't pulled out of the country for safety. As it was, the ambassador told us that an evacuation plan had been drawn up but, to keep the information from falling into the wrong hands, it wouldn't be distributed just yet.

We never did learn those plans. Were we to try to reach the coast where the U.S. Navy might pick us up? Or were we to try to make our way over the mountains into Argentina? Didn't matter, I guess. We were still without a car.

Then bombs were found on the doorsteps of three diplomatic families. None exploded, but the danger was obvious. All of us began checking our yards every morning before allowing children and pets outside.

Saboteurs used dynamite to blow up two main power towers, leaving half the *country* without electricity. And the government banned the sale of the international edition of *Time* magazine, in angry response to reports about food shortages and social unrest in the capital city. Things really were coming unglued.

As we recall, it was in July when the first major tremor shook the status quo. A Chilean army colonel chose to make a statement of disagreement with Salvador Allende's Socialist government. Leading a battalion of tanks under his command, Col. Souper headed for the Moneda Palace in downtown Santiago, around the corner from the embassy.

They left their post on the outskirts of the city and rumbled toward the palace. It was during rush hour that morning and the tanks got caught up in the traffic. They stopped for red lights! Actually, we've always thought that if the tanks had pressed the issue, cars would have yielded the right of way.

At any rate, tanks rumbling through the streets of the city galvanized a *lot* of people. Dan remembers guys running full tilt through the hallways outside his office, and someone positively screeching, "What the *hell* is going on?"

Local police and other officials confronted Col. Souper and his tankers. Their signal of protest was not appreciated and they were arrested and imprisoned. But unrest was now on the front burner.

In those few weeks of calm before the storm, we began keeping water in plastic trashcans and one bathtub, just in case. Portable two-way radios were assigned to each person who worked in Dan's office. Even if telephones didn't function during a possible upheaval, the staff could continue to communicate with each other.

Finally it came. It was September 11, 1973. All branches of the military, Army, Navy and Air Force, as well as the local police force, had had enough. They no longer could accept the unraveling of the Chilean social fabric, the inadequate, blundering and ever more leftist leadership of Allende and his government.

It started out as a normal day. Dan went in to the embassy as usual. Someone had a "source" within the military and word spread quickly through the office. "This looks like it. Everything is about to blow."

Around eight o'clock, the Chilean army moved into the center of the city. As with Col. Souper before them, their main focus was the Moneda Palace. Allende was already in his office there, and word was sent to him that his resignation and surrender were demanded. Col. Souper himself was on hand. Fellow officers secured his release from prison that morning and restored him to his command.

With Allende's immediate, defiant refusal to surrender, gunfire broke out between his component of bodyguards and soldiers surrounding the palace. Listening to the escalating gun battle outside, Dan grabbed the telephone and called me at home to give warning about what was underway.

"For heaven's sake, don't let Penn go to school!" he directed. "Stop the school bus and see if you can contact Sarah. She has to stop David's bus, too. I'll try to be in touch later. Turn on the two-way radio. Maybe you can get some information that way."

Within minutes of his call, the bus arrived to carry Penn off to school. After hearing my frantic words, the driver turned the bus around and retraced his route, returning a dozen children to the safety of their homes. I tried to telephone our friend Sarah, another embassy wife who lived about six blocks away. Her phone service was already out, so I ran as fast as I could, arriving just in time to stop the second bus.

On my jog back home, I went down a street lined with comfortable, well-kept brick houses. As I chuffed past them earlier, all was quiet. Now, though, only a few minutes later, there was a decided difference. Windows and doors of the homes had been thrown open and someone was playing a recording of the Chilean national anthem, loudly, for all to hear.

Residents of the houses had poured out into the street and they were congregating in excitement and hugging each other. And, at not yet nine o'clock in the morning, men were carrying bottles of wine and champagne and trays of glasses out to their neighbors. Shouting "Viva Chile!" one man grabbed me in a bear hug, then spun me around and made a broad, sweeping gesture with his arm. Appearing from the upper windows of houses all along the street,

Chilean flags, featuring one red stripe, one white stripe and a single white star on a field of blue, hung with pride and hope. Clearly, these people were supportive of a change in government.

Meanwhile, back in the city center, the battle was expanding in volume and scope. With Allende's continued refusal to surrender, the army pulled back and the air force took over. One after another, jet fighters screamed over the tops of the buildings and aimed rockets directly at the palace. It went on and on, the thunder of the powerful aircraft punctuated by enormous explosions. A noteworthy fact of that bombardment is that not a single rocket went awry. Each held to its intended course and only the palace was subject to the impacts.

As the rocket attack ran its course, left-wing supporters of the Allende government, directed by foreign communist advisors, filtered into the center of the melee. Now a full-scale battle erupted at street level between the army and the communist urban guerrillas. Automatic machine gun fire became a constant background noise up in Dan's office.

As stray rounds came flying through windows and crashing through workings of air conditioning units, embassy staffers hit the floor and crawled to the safer confines of hallways. In Dan's part of the embassy, a number of people gathered in the vault, a secure area built with extra-thick walls, no windows and a heavy duty, bulletproof door.

Helicopter gunships appeared just above window level, and fighting intensified. After one bullet ricocheted around the office next to Dan's, then landed, spent, in the middle of his friend Dave's desk, Dan and a couple of helpers pushed heavy four-drawer safes against windows for added protection.

Back at the house, our maid Maria was in the living room listening to a local radio station. Allende was broadcasting a drunken-sounding, rambling monologue, which seemed to make little sense. I was upstairs, getting bits and pieces of information from voices coming through the two-way radio. Suddenly, a horrendous noise sent me flying down the stairs and out into the yard.

The air force jets were finished with the Moneda Palace and now were mounting an attack on Allende's residence, eight blocks from our house. They flew in a straight line, just feet above the tall Lombardy poplar trees that grew along the edge of our yard. The vibrations hit me from above, then pounded through my legs, as the energy thundered down into the earth and echoed back again.

Of course, the kids gathered around, wondering what was happening. Little Sam shook four-year-old fists at the jets and yelled, "Cuidado! Cuidado!" (Careful! Careful!)

We stood together and watched in fascinated shock as rockets were released just over our heads and went streaking off ahead of the planes. As the jets flew in a big circle, preparing for another attack, the kids ran for their toy cowboy guns and made a game of aiming at the Hawker Hunters roaring by again, one after another.

Briefly, I thought about sending the kids into the house for safety, but if a rocket tumbled free and fell into our yard, as sturdy and secure as the walls of the house seemed to be, they surely wouldn't offer true protection. So, the kids continued to run back and forth across the lawn, caught up in the awful whirlwind of political upheaval.

The sounds of gun battles in the streets of the center of that city of three million continued in an unpredictable ebb and flow. Gradually, it tapered off. Sometime in the afternoon, around three or four o'clock, a two-hour cease-fire was announced. All those caught in offices or otherwise away from home had a chance to return to their houses before a twenty-four hour curfew went into effect. A skeleton staff was chosen to remain at the embassy. Dan was among those lucky enough to head for home. Boy! Was I glad to see him!

For the next four days, the twenty-four hour curfew, called a "toque de queda," remained in place. Any unauthorized person moving around on the streets during that time faced intense attention by military and police forces spread out through the city. It was *not* a good idea to risk breaking the curfew.

We knew there were those foolhardy enough to do so, however. Starting that very first night, we heard gun battles, and the sounds carried for blocks in the still hours of the darkness. Explosions of heavier artillery, from tanks and bazookas, mixed with machine gun and rifle fire, woke us nightly for weeks.

After the violence of the coup, everyone's nerves were a bit on edge so the huge earthquake that struck later that week was particularly distressing. I heard it coming, as usual, but Dan didn't, as usual. Instantly awake, I shook him and announced, "An earthquake is coming!"

Ever practical, his reply was to the point, "What do you want me to do about it?"

Reflecting the ongoing chaos, the earthquake that night was a terremoto. In Spanish, earthquakes can be either "temblors" or "terremotos." Temblors are garden-variety shakings but terremotos are the big guys.

It came with a fury, rocking the house back and forth as though it would never stop. The noise that arrived with it sounded like a giant train roaring by, just outside our windows. Its aftershocks strong and frequent, we counted over twenty five significant paroxysms that night and a hundred more in the following days.

All of it was enough to unnerve three-year old Kinley. On her own, she worked out an explanation for the shaking. Holding wiggling fingers at either side of her forehead, she proclaimed, "A big monster lives in the ground. He is a 'nerth clake' and he likes to eat little kids. When he gets hungry, he tries to climb out of the ground and he makes our house jump. I hide under my covers."

After the four-day respite, Dan returned to work. At first his days were truncated due to curfew hours, but gradually they returned to normal. For about a week, it wasn't at all unusual for Dan to see bodies in the street. Once, hurrying around a corner, he tripped over a body sprawled on the sidewalk. Nearer home, three incidents of fighting erupted during the early days, one battle taking place only a block away from the house.

As the days passed, the curfew gradually eased. Lifted at six o'clock in the morning, it was reinstated at six in the evening, then seven, then eight o'clock. We adjusted to it and life went on. We even went to a few dinner parties during those days. It was kind of crazy. We sat down to dinner, enjoyed a good-humored get together that helped work out some of the stressful kinks. Then someone checked the clock. "Hey! Half an hour till curfew!" And we raced out the front door, grabbing our dessert, wrapped in napkins and waiting on a tray, as we left.

November approached and the southern hemisphere spring evenings lengthened. Dan and I sat out on the patio and sipped our iced tea. The house was only a couple of blocks from a major intersection and when the minutes closed in on the curfew hour, we braced ourselves. Too many people left too little time for their race toward home. Someone *always* tried to run the red light at that intersection. The squeal of brakes, followed by a heavy crunch was an almost-nightly occurrence.

Eventually embassy personnel, whose duties required them to respond to call-ins during the night, were issued safe passage identification cards, called "salvoconductos." A European diplomat, driving to his embassy one night, was stopped by a military sentry. As the diplomat reached for his wallet to retrieve his salvoconducto, the nervous soldier misinterpreted the action. He shot the man. It was not a fatal incident, but certainly an object lesson for everyone else.

Thereafter, whenever Dan had to go to the embassy during curfew hours, he made it a point to drive very slowly with all windows open so he could hear any order to halt. He also kept the overhead light on, so an observer could see him clearly, and he carried his ID card clenched in his front teeth. That way he never had to reach for it.

Some neighbors were especially happy to learn that Dan carried a safe passage card. They called late one night and asked for his help. He drove the pregnant lady and her husband to the hospital where she delivered her first baby.

A month after the coup, with roads into the city now open, our car and household effects finally were delivered to us. We didn't unpack right away, though. Dan had to attend a conference in Panama, so the kids and I flew with him as far as Quito. We stayed with good friends there until he joined us later in the week.

On our third day in Quito, our hosts Peg and Phil invited a group of other friends over for a cookout. We all were enjoying the get together until children at a house down the block began to set off firecrackers. Hearing the small explosions, I immediately thought of gunfire and instinct took over.

Leaping to my feet, I called, "Kids! Quick! Into the house! *Run!*" Not pausing to ask questions, the kids scampered inside like frightened bunnies. Obviously, the coup affected us more than we realized. We desperately needed that week of R and R.

When we returned to Santiago, Dan and I noticed that the kids spent more time drawing pictures than usual. Soldiers, planes, bombs, helicopters ... They found a way to get the worries out of their systems. They talked it out, too. I still can hear little voices asking, "Remember when we were in the war, Mom?"

Good changes did follow the chaos. The city no longer blockaded, we finally got out to drive around and see some of that beautiful country. People began working again, supermarkets and other shops filled their shelves for the first time in nearly a year and the city took on a clean and vibrant look.

As for the curfew, a short one, from one o'clock until five o'clock every morning, still existed when we moved away from Chile two years later.

◄○►

Eventually we established a normal pattern of life in Santiago and we were about midway through our stay there when Kinley offered up some excitement. Finally, she got to go to school with the boys. By now, Penn was a big second grader, Sam was in kindergarten and Kinley spent every morning in the pre-school class. She loved school, she loved her teacher Mrs. Lyons (though at least half the time she called her "Mr. Tiger"), and she loved spending time with the other children in her class.

Being the little one in the family, Kinley was concerned with things being "fair." It was fair if everyone got the same size cookie. It was fair if everyone had the same bedtime. It wasn't fair that Penn and Sam got to stay at school three hours longer than she did. She tried hiding in the bushes next to the school so she wouldn't have to get on the bus and go home. But the teachers found her and after that they tried to keep a watchful eye on her.

One day Kinley and her classmate Michael got on the Volkswagen van school bus with the other children. But they didn't take their seats as usual. They decided to hide from the driver. Maybe he would deliver the other kids to their homes, then return to school where they could play some more. So Kinley and Michael climbed over the back seat and curled up on the floor in the cozy little spot at the very back.

The hum of the tires on the street, the gentle swaying of the bus, the warm sunshine pouring through the back window onto two quiet little bodies lulled them to sleep in a matter of minutes.

The driver followed his usual route and dropped off the children one by one. He didn't see Kinley and Michael. He didn't know they were there. When the bus was empty— or so he thought— he headed home, across the huge city of Santiago, for lunch. He didn't have to be back at the school for nearly three hours.

Meanwhile, I kept checking the clock and stood by the door as I waited for the bus to stop in front of our gate. When it was half an hour beyond Kinley's usual arrival time, I finally called the school. "Is there something wrong with the bus?" I asked. "Kinley isn't home yet."

And so a flurry of activity, telephone calls and deep concern was unleashed. Teachers at the school beat the bushes looking for Kinley. Not there. They checked every classroom, every closet. Not there, either. The director of the school had not been notified of a traffic accident involving the bus so he telephoned the home of every child who rode the bus that day. He asked if the children arrived home as usual. Were they on time? By chance, did Kinley get off the bus with them?

Interestingly, no one missed Michael. His mother worked part-time at the embassy and sometimes she picked him up from school. When the director called Michael's house, the maid assumed that the little boy was with his mother, and she reported that all was well.

As the minutes dragged by, as telephone calls flew between the school and our house, between the school and other homes, between me and Dan in his office, the bus driver pulled to a stop in front of his house. He got out and walked around the back of the bus toward the sidewalk. Out of the corner of his eye, he noticed something bright yellow behind the back seat. Looking in, he saw two sleeping children. One of them was Kinley in a yellow sun suit. For that man, it was like a jolt of electricity! He ran back to the door of the bus, jumped in and began a hurried delivery of the wayward ones.

While he drove pell mell through the streets of Santiago, we continued to wonder, "Where is she? Did she manage to wander away from the school alone, somehow? Is there any possibility she has been kidnapped?" In the year after the coup against the Allende government, social unrest had been quieted, and life in the Chilean capital was nearing a normal, pleasant flow. Even so, special police guards still patrolled the streets outside the school, machine guns at the ready. They were there in case any terrorist group tried to strike out at the Chilean and/or U.S. government, through the children.

An hour and a half after our preschooler should have been home, we decided it was time to notify the embassy security office that Kinley was missing. Soon, police throughout the city would be looking for the school bus, the driver and a three-year-old American girl in a yellow sun suit. I hung up the phone after talking with Dan. As he walked down the hall in the embassy toward the stairs on his way to the security office, I returned to my post at our front door, watching for the bus to stop at the gate.

Just then, in a cloud of dust and with a screech of brakes, there it was! Leaving Kinley and Michael still sleeping, the driver bolted out of the bus, opened the gate and threw his arms above his head. "No me culpa! No me culpa!" he screamed. "It's not my fault! It's not my fault!" As I hurried to join him, ready to get right in his face, he pointed at the back of the bus.

Seeing the two sleeping babes, I immediately understood what had happened. Assuring the driver that all was forgiven, I watched as he opened the back door and we woke the sleepy heads. I took Kinley in my arms while the driver carried Michael to sit beside him in the front seat.

As they drove off toward Michael's house, I went inside, put Kinley on the sofa, and then made a series of phone calls. All's well that ends well, they say, but we sure had a serious talk with Half-Pint that night.

It was in that same school where Penn met his first best friend. His name was Paul and his father was ambassador of the New Zealand embassy. As luck would have it, Paul's family lived just around the corner and down the street from us. Since there were no streets to cross, Penn and Paul were allowed to walk back and forth from house to house to play together. Our house and yard were big; Paul's house and yard were bigger. Between the two homes the little boys had plenty of space to stretch their legs and amuse themselves in imaginative play.

Another thing about Paul's house was special: Paul had a butler. We had a maid and a gardener but Paul's family had a cook, two maids, a couple of gardeners— and the butler. They needed a large household staff because of the amount of representational entertaining they were required to do. However, Paul's family was a relaxed, down to earth bunch and not at all pretentious.

When the servants weren't involved in preparations for entertaining, they were free— encouraged, actually— to make themselves scarce around the house. That helped maintain a more natural family atmosphere in the residence. So sometimes when Penn went to play with Paul, the butler was available to be their companion.

He accompanied them to movies, rescued them when Paul's older brother locked them in a closet, helped them build a fort, then supervised as they had a cookout over a little campfire. Together they built swings in trees and then picked lemons and made lemonade which they sipped as they sat at a table by the pool and played "Go Fish."

Penn loved Paul's butler and couldn't understand why we didn't have someone like him at our house, too. When the time came for both families to leave Chile, Penn was heartbroken at having to part not only with his best friend but with the butler as well.

Like our maid in Ecuador, our Chilean maid was named Maria and she was a darling. Even-tempered and easygoing, she laughed often and sang while she worked. She gently corrected my errors in Spanish and played hide and seek with the kids among the trees and bushes in the yard. She swam with us in the swimming pool and brought us pastel colored fresh eggs, laid by a special variety of chicken, when she returned from visiting her family in the south.

Of all the helpers we ever had, this Maria came closest to becoming part of our family. The kids and I cried when we hugged her one last time, just before we went to the airport to leave Santiago forever.

Our gardener Antonio actually was more than a gardener. Because he also helped us clean the pool and did other chores around the house, like washing windows and fixing drooping shutters, he was called a "mozo." Meaning something like manservant, a mozo in Chile had more status than a gardener. And our mozo, who had been a professional boxer in his younger days, was a man filled with pride and dignity. When he came to work, he arrived wearing a business suit and carried his work clothes in a brief case.

Antonio was great company and an efficient worker. Everything he did was accomplished without wasted energy. He didn't wait to be asked to work on specific chores, but walked around and looked for things to do. Everyone should be lucky enough to have an Antonio pass through his or her life at least once.

When Sam was four years old, he developed a taste for escargot. Or the Chilean equivalent thereof. We didn't know about his culinary daring, though. Honest.

As Antonio worked among the plants and bushes, he collected large-shelled snails called "caracoles." He usually took them home in a plastic bucket for his family table. Sometimes, however, as we were to learn, he cooked up a batch of them on a hot plate in the gardening shed and had them for his lunch.

Sam enjoyed Antonio's company and often "helped" with the yard work. Antonio was the father of four sons of his own and was kind and patient with his little assistant, teaching Sam the names of flowers and bushes. He sometimes "paid" Sam for an afternoon of help by making him a bow and arrow from small, supple branches and a piece of string. Other times he invited Sam to sit with him in the sunshine and have a bite to eat.

Sam loved those snails! We learned about his acquired taste one Saturday afternoon. "Mom! Dad! Make Sam stop!" came the cry.

Sam had located a family of snails in some bushes along one fence and there he sat, prying them out of their shells with a little twig and popping them into his mouth.

We put a stop to that pint-size gourmet's al-fresco dining. At least we think we did.

—◦—

Sometimes raising kids can be a real circus. During our days in Santiago, we went through a period of over three consecutive months when we were tethered to the house because of one *long* run of childhood illnesses.

It started the morning when six-year-old Penn woke up with chicken pox. Before he could return to school, Sam developed the spots and then, before Sam was completely cured, we found the pox upon Kinley.

Actually, this first round wasn't too hard on any of us. We had little bed trays with side pockets. We filled the pockets with little toys and art supplies—crayons, scissors, stickers and paper. The polka-dot child played in bed or sat in the sun in front of a window and stayed busy. We cut sandwiches with animal cutters and did all the things we could to help them forget the itching and make the ailing easier.

Bath time was little Kinley's favorite. First she soaked in a tub in which we dissolved some baking soda, to help dry up the spots. After toweling off came the fun part. We bought some menthol powder from the pharmacy and, using a big fluffy powder puff, Kinley patted every dot. The powder was cool and soothing, the puff was a fancy toy, and the bigger cloud of dust she created, the better.

Before Kinley was finished with the pox, Penn came home with the measles. And so it went. This was getting a little tiresome. We were in the last week with the measles when Sam woke up with the mumps.

Good grief! Will it never end? My interest in catering to, and providing entertainment for, sickly children was beginning to pall. Again we ran the gauntlet, with one child picking up when the other left off.

Finally we were down to just Penn with the mumps. Known in Chile as "the little pig disease," it was an awful case. He was swollen and miserable. But, at last, we said, "Yes, tomorrow you may go back to school."

That morning he hopped out of bed, intending to dress and hurry downstairs. But, wait. Something isn't right. He looked in the mirror—and started screaming.

I rushed into his room and nearly joined in his screams. He had the mumps again! The first round had been only one side, but it was so extreme that the swelling pushed under his jaw and up, making it appear to be a complete case. Now, though, the other side was fully involved. And in the strangest twist, the membrane on the floor of his mouth swelled so much that when he opened his mouth it looked like he had a second tongue. Thank heavens, eventually all returned to normal.

Load it Up, Move it Out

It's behind us now, all those moves and the packing and unpacking. As we relocated from country to country, station to station, we had moving crews in our houses a lot. They either wrapped and boxed things up to carry away, or unloaded our belongings from the big wooden lift vans and carried them into our most recent residence. In all, twenty six different crews became part of our lives— twenty seven, if you count the ones who moved us across town when we lived in Quito.

We learned all sorts of things that made our moves easier but, to be honest, it never got to the point that a move was a breeze. Prior to our first pack-out I had no idea how fast those guys could sweep through a bedroom or empty a set of kitchen cupboards. Anything left in a room where packers are working is fair game to them and I wasn't always ready. That's how a full sugar bowl and a butter dish holding half a stick of margarine were wrapped up "as is" and unpacked in a messy state several months later in Victoria.

That was the same move when the packers grabbed our full kitchen garbage can and sent it into storage for over two years. At least by the time it was delivered to us in Ecuador, the odor was a thing of the past. Luckily we never had to stop the forward progress and hastily unpack box after box in a frantic search for car keys, passports and airplane tickets.

The unpacking exercise was always our preferred part of a move. Once the furniture and boxes were in the right rooms we bid farewell to the moving crews, declining their offers to help unpack. We then could work at our own pace and put things where we thought they logically belonged. It never failed, though, that something got misplaced, not to be seen again until we unpacked somewhere else, two or three years down the line.

Unpacking was also somewhat of a Christmas-y experience for the kids. We always let them empty their own boxes of toys. After several months of not seeing their favorite trucks, dolls and games, they spent happy hours entertaining themselves, rushing into each other's bedrooms with shouts of "Look what I just found!"

During the packout process, however, we always were working against a deadline and the mantra running through our heads was "Be organized, be ready." Generally our belongings had to be separated into three categories: what needed to be sent by airfreight, those items going in a sea shipment and articles being put into storage in a warehouse someplace.

The airfreight was a limited shipment made up of items we needed immediately in a partially furnished temporary apartment at our new post, the basics for setting up a new living situation. We needed dishes, silverware, pots and pans. Sheets, towels and pillows. A clock radio, electric fans, a cookbook, a few games or toys for the kids. That sort of thing.

The sea shipment was comprised of most of our household effects. That was the furniture we would need, rugs, paintings, books, photo albums and Christmas decorations. Those things that make a house a home. The rest of our belongings, things we could live without for a few years, went into storage.

Getting and keeping everything separated was always the big challenge. At the cost of a few more gray hairs each time, we usually were astonishingly successful. Sometimes we tagged items with different colored stickers to identify them— green for airfreight, red for surface, yellow for storage.

More often, we separated things before the packers got to the house. All airfreight went into one specific room and storage things were gathered in the basement. The rest of the stuff in the house was meant to go in the sea shipment.

Most packouts took three full working days to accomplish. But the longest occurred when we were leaving Santiago, Chile. It took nine days. It was more than two years after the coup against Salvador Allende and there had been serious disruption in trade and commerce and real problems with the availability and distribution of goods. When we reached our packout time, there still were unexpected shortages of even the most common supplies.

The moving company had very little tape and a shortage of both wrapping paper and cardboard cartons. The packers did their best, wrapping plates in small bundles with hand-cut corrugated paper and then tying them closed with strings of hemp. It took forever! Sometimes they had to wait for boxes to be emptied at one house and then brought to be filled at ours.

One day, when the workers were at loose ends awaiting delivery of more supplies, they created their own diversion. I came down the stairs in time to see two grown men in a furious race down the length of the adjoining living room and dining room. As their co-workers cheered them on, they were madly peddling away on the kids' tricycles.

We're glad we didn't have to cope with the problem our friends Terry and Cathy faced. When they left Bamako, Mali, there was very little wrapping paper available. Waste paper from local offices was shredded and put to use. Unfortunately, no one culled the paper first and all of their kitchen contents were packed in shredded carbon paper.

Loss and damage of one sort or another are inevitable when people move frequently. All things considered, we were pretty lucky. Once a darling little clock, a gift to us when we announced our engagement, disappeared and a few other items were lost to breakage along the way.

Then there was the car we shipped to Ecuador. It arrived in sorry shape. Somewhere on its journey, the windshield wipers, battery, distributor cap and all four hubcaps were stolen. Then, as it sat in the hold of the ship, a pallet of paint cans was hoisted above it. Some of the cans rolled free and fell. The back window was shattered and the roof was dented like a calypso band's steel drum. We knew paint was in those cans because, adding insult to injury, one broke open and spilled bright yellow enamel over the hood and down the sides of the green car.

Other families faced their own losses. We knew one couple who went to the dock to watch their household effects arrive. As they looked on, their sea-tainer came uncoupled from the crane and all their belongings dropped into the water.

Some other friends were moving into their new quarters and were pleased that the piano had arrived in fine shape. Standing beside the van, one of the moving men let go of it, assuming it was steady enough on the sloping Boli-vian street. It wasn't. It began rolling, gathered speed and finally, with the frantic mother looking on, crashed into a stone retaining wall at the end of the street.

And then there were the Runyans. They arrived in town but their house-hold effects didn't. For two years, the crates were sent from one country to another and back again, with official cables chasing them everywhere. As time passed, the family had to shop for new clothes for everyone, linens, kitchen items and toys for the kids. Their tour drew to a close and a packout date was scheduled for their new belongings. And the wayward shipment arrived at last.

The chaos and upheaval of our moves wasn't limited to just the actual packing and unpacking. In between posts, we returned to the States for home leave, giving us three to six weeks to visit family and friends and quickly reacquaint ourselves with the country and culture we were serving. Sometimes there was a reverse culture-shock aspect associated with our return to the land of plenty. Once we stood on a beach in Florida, watching a group of teenagers play volleyball. All of a sudden I realized tears were rolling down my cheeks. The contrast between the kids in front of us, healthy, happy and privileged, and the children left behind in their Third World hard-scrabble lives was simply too much to think about.

Another time we went to a large department store to buy a swimming suit for Kinley. In the children's section, a particularly spacious area was devoted to rows and rows of racks of swimming suits for little girls. After eight years in South America, we were used to choosing items from a meager availability of goods on the local market. Otherwise, we shopped from Sears and J.C. Penney's catalogs, which provided an adequate but somewhat limited selection.

Now, faced with a virtual plethora of little swimming suits— bikini, tank, ruffles, stripes, polka dots, in all the colors of the rainbow— it was too much. Making a choice was impossible. Excess in itself was limiting. We left the store without buying anything.

Several times we spent part of our home leave shopping for things we would need at our next post. Trips to the supermarket were an adventure for us. Forty, fifty, sixty varieties of breakfast cereals! A whole row of nothing but cookies! People gave us curious looks when they overheard our conversations: "Two rolls of paper towels ought to last a couple of years, but we better get a whole case of this peanut butter."

We bought fifteen or twenty pairs of children's shoes at once. "This shoe in sizes five, six, seven and eight, please," we'd say. "Eventually someone will grow into them."

We also shopped for Christmas and birthday gifts for the next two or three years. "What will the kids want and be ready for down the line? Can we talk Sam into really, really wanting Santa to bring him this little riding tractor next year? Do you think Penn will even know what to do with this funny shaped American football?"

Arrival at a new post was always an adventure. It didn't matter where we stayed during the first few weeks. Just having a place where we could relax was enough. After all, we'd just gone through the hard work of a packout, plus the rush and upheaval of travel.

Sometimes we stayed in embassy-provided temporary quarters and twice we stayed in hotels. Other times we went directly from the airport to our new home. As I say, it didn't matter. Since everything around us was new and strange, those early days were almost like being on vacation. But eventually we settled into a new routine.

◄◦►

At last our tours in South America came to an end. Eight years after leaving the States, we were going home. And, boy, were we in for a dose of reality!

We bought a new four-bedroom house in a suburban development full of look-alike center hall colonial style homes. People worked compulsively on their lawns, keeping grass free of weeds and planting colorful azalea bushes and flowering dogwood trees. Neighbors gathered outside and watched the kids race bicycles, tricycles and big wheels up and down the sidewalks. It looked like Easy Street to us.

The movers finished carrying our furniture into the house and we hurried to put things away. We were eager to get settled so we could be part of the neighborhood, too. We didn't know it yet, but actually we were something like fish out of water. In a way, the transition was easier for Dan than it was for the kids and me.

He found his way to the hardware store and garden center, adding words like "spackle" and "mulch" to his vocabulary. He built a handsome patio behind the house, then sported bandages like suburban badges after sawing deeply into one finger and vigorously hammering another. Then he went back to work at CIA Headquarters in Langley, Virginia, and left the kids and me to enjoy our exciting new life.

Penn, Sam and Kinley were American almost in name only. They talked about the U.S. as "home," yet they'd never lived here. They had no frame of reference for fitting into the flow of life in small town Virginia.

Because they always had lived behind fences, they were shy about leaving our yard at first, but once they understood that all the kids ran free up and down the block, they assumed that everything was communal property. We spent one week teaching them that other people's flowers were not fair game for picking. And there was more learning yet to come.

All three understood English perfectly, yet early on they had settled on Spanish as the language they used when playing. As they got to know the neighborhood kids, they spoke English to their new friends but called out to each other in Spanish. That always stopped the game in progress. It was like they were "cheating," talking with words the others didn't understand, almost in a secret code. They didn't mean to be different. In fact, they desperately wanted to belong. Very shortly, they dropped their Spanish entirely.

Their foreignness showed up in other ways. Sometimes they said things like, "The boats that go through the Panama Canal are bigger than your house," and "the guards at our school had real machine guns." Or they asked in all seriousness, "Doesn't anyone here have a butler?" They weren't showing off or trying to act like jet-set kids. They spoke of the only background they knew. And it was decidedly different. Those awkward times soon passed, however, and the kids began to blend into their new life.

Meanwhile, Mom was having a struggle of her own.

Once we got used to having maids around the house all the time, it was easy to take their help for granted. We tried to keep in mind that we were living in temporary luxury and eventually would return to the "real world." We really didn't want to take all the foofaraw too seriously.

But I had never been a U.S. housewife and for eight years someone else vacuumed the floors and dusted the furniture. They washed the windows and cleaned the bathrooms. They made it look so easy. The houses always were clean, tidy and inviting. It can't be *that* hard, I concluded. What I failed to consider was the fact that that was their job— and it was the only thing they did.

And so, from the very first, I threw myself at housewifery perfection. Every day I vacuumed and sprayed Pledge, cleaned the tubs, mopped the kitchen floor. Looking out through the sparkling windows, I saw the neighbor ladies chatting in one front yard and then another. How were they cleaning their houses so quickly? I worked faster and faster, trying to complete my routine so I, too, could go outside and visit. Looking again, I saw that the morning gabfest was over and resolved to be more efficient tomorrow.

As the exhausting pace continued, I began to nag the kids. "Don't leave your jacket there! Put your toys away! Who made this mess?" Even I could see that Mom was a lot less fun to be around now that we lived in the States. What was I doing wrong? How did the other moms do all the same work, yet still have time to be friendly and have some fun?

Incredibly, it never occurred to me that their routines and priorities were different than I imagined. There I was, all alone in my time-warp dilemma. I thought Donna Reed and June Cleaver were still alive and well, not knowing that I missed out on a transition somewhere along the line.

And so it went for a month. Then early one evening, in a freak accident, I took a clumsy misstep and fell, breaking both ankle and knee. So much for Mrs. Clean. With the cast on my leg holding me back, the house took on a lived-in look, like the others up and down the street. I stopped nagging the kids so much and, hobbling on crutches, finally went outside to meet the neighbors. It was a tough way to come to grips with reality, but life for all of us was happier after that. We got into the American swing at last.

Golden Days

As Bill Cosby might say, "It was 116 degrees. In the shade. Not a snowball in sight."

We draped ourselves over sofa and chairs, wearing loose shorts and light weight t-shirts, hoping that on its next rotation the pathetic little fan would stir enough air to create a whiff of relief. We were in Athens, Greece. We also were in misery. We were almost too hot to sweat. It really was 116 degrees.

The heat wave hit shortly after we moved into our house. Athens was our fourth overseas post, an assignment that followed three tours in South America and almost two years in Virginia. Our car hadn't arrived in Greece yet so Dan was using an office vehicle to commute between work and home. We had to wait until his off-hours, evenings and weekends, to escape to the beach.

Meanwhile, we cooked. Stepping out onto the balcony didn't make us feel any cooler but it was an interesting experience. Kind of like being inside a popcorn popper. Pinecones on trees around us were bursting open in explosive spurts, expelling seeds to replenish themselves, the way it happens during forest fires.

Finally, it occurred to me to fill the bathtub. It stayed full of water for a long stretch through that summer. Whenever someone got just too hot, it was time for a quick dip. Some nights were almost as bad as the days, so we learned to take a cooling soak then hurry back to bed without drying off. A quick roll in the sheets left them slightly damp and cool, just enough to allow us to get back to sleep.

When the next summer rolled around, we were old hands at dealing with that kind of heat. By the time our good friends Ken and Doris arrived from Maryland to visit us, the tub was full and waiting. Both of them are tall, boisterous and alive with their own brand of effervescence and good humor and we were delighted with their company. We let them in on our secret for cool-down and soon they joined the parade of people wandering around our house in the middle of the night in varying stages of dress and undress.

It was about two o'clock one morning when the phone rang. Ken, Doris, Dan and I met near the telephone, wearing undershorts, a robe, a towel, whatever. Ken's cousin was calling to say that Ken's dad had suffered a heart attack and was in intensive care at the local hospital in Maryland.

"Should we leave Athens and fly home?" they asked.

After discussing the situation, they finally decided to continue their vacation, with the understanding that Ken's cousin would call again if a return home seemed necessary.

The next night, with someone else soaking in the tub, the phone rang again. And again we congregated in our abbreviated costumes at the telephone, all fearing the worst. This time, however, it was Dan's mother, calling to say *his* dad had suffered a heart attack and was in intensive care at the local hospital. In fact, he was in the room next to Ken's dad.

In the end, both men recovered. But it was a mighty coincidence. Two fathers side by side in a hospital, while their sons, who competed against each other in a Beautiful Baby contest thirty five years earlier, were together, in the midst of a brutal heat wave, in a house halfway around the world.

—◁◦▷—

As warm and friendly as we found the Greeks to be, we didn't always understand them, nor were we prepared for their sometimes volatile and unpredictable behavior.

Whenever snow fell in the northern suburbs of Athens and in the hilly countryside beyond, Greeks by the hundreds leaped into their cars and raced madly into the midst of the storm. They stopped along roadsides, in long lines of creative parking jobs, and staged enthusiastic and vigorous snowball fights. Many of them were clad in business suits and wore slippery-soled dress shoes, which only added to the comical picture.

When they tired of their play, they turned to serious work: the job of building personal, portable snowmen on the hoods of their cars. Some built their snowmen around radio antennas, using the metal rod as a sort of anchor. Others fashioned their snowmen in the center of the hood, directly in front of the windshield, and hoped for the best as they returned to the city bearing proof of their day in the snow.

One afternoon we witnessed the demise of one such snowman and the chaotic aftermath of the accident. The kids and I were walking along in an area of shops near our house when we approached an intersection. The driver of a car traveling along a side street ignored the stop sign and entered the intersection, directly into the path of another car that was carrying a very large snowman. Both drivers slammed on their brakes and the cars came to a stop with bumpers only inches apart. The force of the sudden braking catapulted the snowman off the hood and through the air to a landing spot six feet away. Naturally, it smashed to smithereens.

The two drivers jumped out of their cars and the owner of the snowman began a furious dance. He hopped up and down in a frenzy, screaming and waving his arms at the pile of snow in the middle of the otherwise dry intersection. The other driver yelled back, and soon the two were engaged in a wild fistfight.

Traffic came to a halt and other drivers approached the action. Without prompting, half a dozen of the watchers became participants. Some grabbed hunks of snow and smashed it over heads of those nearby and soon they were grappling with each other and falling to the asphalt in enthusiastic wrestling matches.

We watched the melee in fascinated amazement until it ended as suddenly as it began. All the drivers returned to their cars and traffic moved again, as though nothing had happened.

Some months later we witnessed another impromptu exhibition of wrestling, their ancient national sport. Next door to our house a large apartment building was being built and a deep cistern was dug along one side, adjacent to our yard. Apparently the idea was to line the walls of the cistern with brick. One afternoon a truck backed into the space, carrying a load of bricks. The driver miscalculated and, instead of unloading the bricks several feet away, he dumped the entire load into the cistern.

It took several days for the workers to carry the bits and pieces up their rickety ladder. They tossed broken bricks into a pile on one side of the hole and piled whole, usable ones on the other side. Since there weren't enough bricks to do the job, another truck eventually arrived and a second load was safely dumped.

Not ten minutes after that truck departed, the kids called to me from the balcony off our living room. "Mom! Come quick! Look at what's happening!" Yet another truck had arrived, carrying a huge load of sand. Again, the driver had poor aim and he covered the usable bricks with a ton of white sand. And the entire small man-made mountain was alive with screaming workers, pushing, shoving and clobbering each other as they rolled in the sand and vented their frustrations.

◄○►

Although we didn't have a maid in Athens, we did have a gardener. He came with the house. The landlord employed him to care for the spectacular roses that set off the yard and what a gardener he was! He kept the blooms coming from March through December, though the roses were at their best in the spring. We lived on a corner lot and the bushes lined the fence at the front of the yard and along the side. People often stopped their cars and picked bouquets of the blooms that hung over the fence. One woman even came into the yard to do her picking. Bold as brass, she came with her shears and a basket about once a month. She just opened the gate, walked in and helped herself. It got to the point that whenever I saw her I wanted to yell, "Go away!" But, in truth, since there were so many roses, we really didn't miss what she took.

◄○►

Odd behavior by the Greeks aside, that tour in Athens was a happy time for us. We took advantage of every opportunity to play at the beaches and visit nearby islands. In an almost osmosis-like process, the kids absorbed the stories of Greek mythology and ancient history. Actually, just being there was a living history lesson.

Our favorite beach, the one nearest our house, was a short drive away, over the hills and down a curvy road, on the Bay of Marathon. From our first weeks in the country, we took full advantage of that beach. Late in the afternoon, the kids gathered together swimming gear and towels, beach chairs and mats, while I packed a picnic dinner. We were dressed and ready when Dan got home from work. As he changed, we loaded the car and then we were off.

It wasn't long before the kids knew well the story of the Battle of Marathon, how the Persians sailed into the bay and landed at "our" beach. The Athenians beat them back and a Greek soldier ran the twenty six miles from

Marathon to the city, carrying news of the victory. The original Marathon Run.

Nearby, we located the monument to the fallen Greek warriors, situated in a grove of almond trees, and even gained access to the nearby burial mound. Inside the tomb, a few graves had been opened, then covered with glass lids. Not only were there skeletons of warriors, complete with metal helmets and shields, but the skeletons of two horses killed during the fighting were displayed as well. Seeing those things, being on the spot, really caught the kids' imaginations.

◄○►

Of the holidays we spent overseas, Easters in Greece remain among our favorites. Maybe that's because there were twice as many Easters in that country as in other places we lived. There was Western Easter as well as the Orthodox celebration and usually they didn't coincide.

One Orthodox Easter morning we woke to a warm, beautiful day. It was perfect for a picnic at the beach. We grabbed odds and ends out of refrigerator and cupboards and packed the cooler. The kids, who now were in elementary school, dug snorkels and fins out of the closet and stuffed towels and swim suits into tote bags. Everyone and everything loaded into the car, we headed out. We decided to visit the nearby small island of Euboea.

Separated from the mainland only by a narrow channel, spanned by a small sturdy bridge, Euboea offered us an easy day trip off the beaten path, where we found an interesting variety of places to enjoy.

Of course, there were beaches. Some were pebbly, where the seabed was covered by odd pods, homes for the ugly sea snails we liked to look at through our masks. Some were smooth and sandy and others were like sandstone flats, where puddles were left in irregular depressions at low tide.

One time we discovered, in some interconnecting puddles, strange little sea animals we never saw before or since. They were flat, amoeba-shaped blobs with arm-like projections and little faces that looked like they were smiling at us.

Too bad we don't have a photo of us from that day. All of us were lying on our stomachs, peering into the puddle, noses close to the surface of the water, examining the strange little things. We must have looked like thirsty refugees, lapping up life-giving liquid at a desert oasis.

But we found more than just beaches on Euboea. On a hill near the town of Chalkis are the ruins of an ancient Turkish fort. When we visited the fort, the kids used their shoes to scuff outlines of their make-believe headquarters in the dusty courtyard. Then they raced away to "man the ramparts," where they searched for an imaginary enemy force preparing to attack.

Inside the fort were domed ceilings, arched windows and doors, and spooky recesses never penetrated by sunlight. In the harsh and stony atmosphere, stalactites were beginning to drip downward in the gloom. The kids chose one particularly dark little room as their hide and seek "jail." They liked running from room to room, stalking each other, while Dad liked stepping out of dark corners and scaring their socks off.

Just down the coast from the fort were even more ancient ruins. At the edge of the site, a team of archaeologists was working at uncovering two lovely mosaic floors. That particular area was fenced off, but on each visit we leaned against the poles and checked their progress. We delighted in the successive areas being exposed for the first time in hundreds, perhaps thousands, of years.

Another part of the site featured the remains of a gymnasium and the baths. Large stone basins ran in a line along a sloping hill and whenever we walked by them, the kids each chose one, hopped in and pretended to scrub away the fine Greek dust.

Best of all was the outdoor amphitheater. Only a few stone seats remained on the curving terraces. The rest probably had been used as building blocks for the cottages in the nearby village. In the "backstage" part of the open theater, steps led down to the still-standing stone tunnel from which actors emerged onto the stage.

Hardly anyone ever visited the site because it wasn't a major ruin, nor was it on the usual tourist path. We came to think of the theater almost as "ours." While Dan and I were attentive audience, the kids sang, danced, made speeches and staged enthusiastic sword fights.

Had they joined us in the audience, one wonders what the ancient Greeks would have thought of Penn's enthusiastic rendition of "I Want a Hippopotamus for Christmas." What's a hippopotamus? For that matter, what's Christmas?

On that particular Orthodox Easter morning, we chose to travel in a loop, starting by driving to the ferryboat landing where we boarded a noisy, vibrating car ferry for the ride to Euboea. We made our rounds, visiting each of the ruins in turn. After enjoying our picnic lunch on the amphitheater's terrace, looking out toward the sea, we made our way to the beach for an afternoon of water fun.

Several hours later, we toweled ourselves dry and drove to the fort, then over the bridge and back to the mainland. As we headed down the road toward Athens, we passed what had been the harbor where ancient Greeks gathered their fleet to sail off to rescue Helen of Troy. Just beyond the harbor, about a mile down the road, we noticed a family gathered outside in the sunshine, preparing their Easter dinner.

They made a perfect tableau. A blue wooden door was balanced on two large barrels for their table. Wooden boxes, kegs and an assortment of kitchen chairs were placed around the table to seat the crowd. As the men enjoyed their glasses of ouzo, they leaned back against the wall of an old stone barn. Two women, dressed in traditional black, were off to one side, turning the spits on which two lambs were roasting over a charcoal pit.

As we passed the gathering, we realized what a wonderful photograph they would make. So we slowed, made a U-turn in the road and drove back. Camera now in hand, I held it out the window, making a pantomimic request for permission to photograph them. Understanding immediately, they beamed and nodded their heads in agreement.

I hopped out of the car and snapped a couple of pictures. Just then a young man approached and, using what English he knew, invited us to join them. Appreciating the invitation but reluctant to intrude, we thanked him but declined. He repeated the invitation and was backed by murmurs and gestures from the others in the family.

Not wanting to appear rude, we finally agreed to sit with them for a little while. They were delighted to share their Easter celebration and quickly made room for Dan and me. A few children smiled shyly and made hand motions, wanting our kids to join them in a game of "Let's chase the chickens."

We had a lovely time. The table held plates of Greek salad, made with pieces of ripe tomato, cucumber, onions and olives and big chunks of fresh feta cheese. Bowls were full of traditional Orthodox Easter eggs, all dyed bright red. And on a tray were hunks and slices of lamb, fresh from the roasting pit. The family fetched plates for us, too, and soon we were eating their feast with them, our conversation assisted by the young man acting as translator for our less-than-fluent attempts at Greek.

We wanted to contribute to the table, but had little left in our cooler. Even so, we excused ourselves and went to the car to see what remained from our picnic. We came up with two cans of cold beer, two of ginger ale, an unopened package of Oreo cookies and a bottle of catsup, all purchased at the U.S. military commissary in Athens. As generous in spirit as in fact, the family acted as though our meager contribution were the "piece de resistance" of the meal.

We enjoyed their company and hospitality but finally had to continue on our way. While we thanked our new friends and shook hands all around, the young man ran across the road to a small white house fitted with the usual blue shutters and door. There, he filled a jar with the family's supply of homemade retsina wine. He carried it back to us and pressed the gift into Dan's hand. And he thanked *us* for making the day special!

—◄o►—

For a while I had trouble with the simple Greek words "yes" and "no." No is "oxi," pronounced "oh hee" and yes is "neh." The words should have been easy enough to remember, but oxi was pretty close to our okay and neh logically corresponded to no in my mind.

One afternoon while out doing errands, I attempted a shortcut, which took me down a narrow dirt road very close to the open front doors of several poor shanties. I was driving a vehicle rarely seen there at that time. It was a new, full size Chevrolet Blazer, with extra wide tires. As I approached the houses, several small children came dashing out and began running alongside the truck, much like little dogs chasing a car.

I slowed to a crawl, just inching along, and the children began patting the side of the Blazer and reaching out to touch the tires. Alarmed, and wanting them to move away, I came to a stop and called out the window to them, "Neh! Neh!" Encouraged by my inadvertent approval, they then climbed up onto the hood, perhaps wanting to take a ride.

It was several minutes before I was able to attract the attention of their parents, who seemed pleased that I had invited the children to enjoy a new playground. Eventually the little ones were removed and I was able to continue on my way, chagrined but no longer confused over "oxi" and "neh."

—◄o►—

If we'd had a lick of sense, we would have carried a revolving door with us when we moved. For all those people who were just passing through, as well as visitors who moved in, unpacked and stayed for months.

We remember those times when one bunch bid us adieu in the morning and there was just time enough to change sheets on the beds before the next wave came through the door in the afternoon. Worse yet were the few occasions when visitors overlapped briefly and they politely snapped and snarled at each other, jealously vying for our time and attention.

Generally, we enjoyed having them come. We knew that their overseas trips were something special, experiences worth remembering. We tried to add to their memories by taking them to places off the beaten path where they could see and do things the ordinary tourist misses.

When Dan's parents visited us in Athens, we easily assumed our familiar role as tour guides. Something special was on the agenda each day. Gramma and Grandad were interested in the blends they found there. Both ancient and modern, it isn't quite European, nor is it Middle Eastern.

Construction of homes and buildings was going on everywhere. Likewise, ruins left from the Golden Age of Greece were visible both in the middle of the city as well as throughout the rocky countryside. They commented to us that it seemed like everything was either going up or coming down.

On one of our sightseeing trips with them, we drove along the coastal road, south from Athens toward the ancient Temple of Poseidon at Sounion. The ride was a treat for all of us, three generations squeezed shoulder to shoulder in family togetherness.

We followed the jagged shore, seeing at every turn a succession of beautiful views. Small islands in the distance appeared and disappeared, and we spotted big ships on the horizon. Small fishing boats sailed on smooth water beyond the foaming waves that beat against the rocks. Wild flowers joined in our celebration of the day, nodding colorful heads along both sides of the road.

The white marble sanctuary is, in fact, a roofless skeleton, the remnants of what once was a complete and magnificent temple dedicated to Poseidon, god of the sea. Enough of it remains for it to be immediately recognized as a vestige of ancient history. Built on the highest part of the promontory, it stands out against the blue sky and is visible for miles as visitors approach. It is a breathtaking scene.

As we neared the parking lot, we momentarily lost sight of the temple as the rocky hillside blocked our view. Grandad got out of the car, hitched up his pants, and smoothed his white hair. Then he turned his gaze to the white columns standing above us in the golden Greek sunshine.

"Hmmm," he mused. "I wonder what they're building up there."

—◦—

Growing up overseas, far away from grandparents, aunts, uncles and cousins, the kids were encouraged from the earliest possible time to keep in touch through letters. We never were concerned with correcting their spelling errors, figuring that would improve over time. The important thing was for them to work on their English and just get their thoughts on paper.

Many of their letters so delighted the family that they were passed around at picnics and Sunday dinners, then carefully saved. We're glad they survived. Occasionally we drag them out and are charmed again, particularly by six- year old Kinley's happy chatter.

> *Dear Granmo*
>
> *I miss you very much. I can not wate tell we come home. We want to go up to Yellwe Ston Porck.*
>
> *I am having a good time in Grees. All are rosis are brnt bee cuz it is hot.*
>
> *Sam had a nise berthday and he got a skate borde and a pump for too bolls wat he got for his berthday.*
>
> *We went to the sawnd and lite showe. Soree you coont cum.*
>
> *Love Kinley*

> *Dear unckl Tim*
>
> *Wen we went to the beech Sam fawnd a see hors and it was green. Ken and Doaris are heer. Ken fawnd a star fish and my dad fawnd six starfish and I dint find enee. Did you no my Grandad had a hard tack?*
>
> *I hoppe he is are ite.*
>
> *Love Kinley*

Dear Grandad

I hoppe you will get well soon and ceap hellthy and weer sory you
are in the hospitll. We cant wate to go home to see you a gen.

Ken is tilingus jocs and wen he was tring to teech us haw to wisall
I coont doo it beecus I lost a nuther tooth. And the one I lots wen you
wer heer dint cum in yet. I hoppe you wont diy.

Love Kinley

Dear Gramo

I am sad beecus Grandad had a hard tack. I hoppe he gets beter.
I sent alleter to him and I hoppe he well feel beter wen it gets ther.

I mis cuming to your hows and staying over nite. And going awt
to coffee with you.

Can you find sum facke fyger nayolse for me? Tell are cusins thet
we mis them.

It is getting nis and cold. We donte have much time to swimm.

Love Kinley

Sometimes it took a while, but the family always managed to decipher her writings. The biggest challenge was figuring out her request for some red-tipped fake finger nails she wanted to use when playing dress-up. And, yes, she finally learned to spell in a more traditional way.

◄○►

When we moved to Greece, maybe we should have bought a TV. As it was, the kids were dependent upon their imaginations for entertainment. We went through phases. For a while, Dan and I were drafted to be their evening audience. We watched one puppet show after another. Then it was "TV news." Clad in costumes dragged out of their dress-up basket, Penn acted as anchorman, Sam covered sports and Kinley told us about make-believe weather disasters that plagued the world.

Ultimately they moved on to pretend games out on the balcony. Inviting little school pals from blocks around, they set up shop as barbers. They collected nearly-empty bottles of after shave lotion, safety razors (minus blades), old shaving brushes and hair combs. Their white terry cloth bathrobes were donned by whoever opted to be barber of the day.

The game was ongoing and continued for a couple of weeks. The other kids pitched in. They stacked small boxes for cabinets and filled them with perfume samples, shaving foam, bath powder and puffs. Customers read comic books as they waited for their turn in one of the lawn chairs and then paid with green figs picked from the tree in the back yard. Rarely had our children and their friends smelled so good or had such clean and shining faces and well-combed hair.

It all came to an end the afternoon one of the visiting kids brought a pair of forbidden scissors. Yes, I should have seen it coming. But I really thought they understood the rules. I think it was eight of them who spent the remainder of the summer growing out the ragged, jagged hairstyles that resulted.

Next they moved on to engineering. Our house was built so that it rested on stilts, big concrete columns. The space under the house was a shady area where we parked the car at night, and where the kids played during the day. The problem with the house being upstairs was that groceries had to be toted a long way from the car to the kitchen.

The kids disliked having to help haul the bags of food all the way up the stairs. There *had* to be a better way! One day they gathered all the ropes they could find, plus a sturdy cardboard box. They referred to the contraption as their elevator. They worked and worked, trying to figure out how to keep the box from tipping and how to make the ropes pull smoothly.

Late in the afternoon it was time for a trial run. How much weight could they handle? I was in the kitchen, starting dinner, when I heard the shriek of terror. Rushing out the front door, I found Penn and Sam, red faced and pulling on the ropes as hard as they could. Dangling just below the edge of the balcony was Kinley, head downward, arms flailing, and yelling as loud as she could.

Settling their sister in the box, the boys had tied the ends of the ropes to each of her ankles to sort of anchor her and then began the old heave-ho. As the elevator rose, it jerked, tipped and quickly spilled its occupant. The empty box now slapped against the back of Kinley's legs.

Afraid she would fall and break her neck, I hurried down to stand just under her, and then firmly directed the boys to ease her down— gently. Back on the ground, she suffered only purple bruises around the top of each foot. Penn and Sam were sentenced to apologize to their little sister and give her a hug. They also had to spend the rest of our stay in Greece with no elevator to help out on grocery days.

When we decided to become gardeners we dug up a small plot behind the house. We mixed fertilizer into the soil, lined up the rows and hopefully planted the seeds. We referred to our small vegetable garden as the South Forty.

On this particular day, I was weeding the South Forty.

When I went outside, the kids were in their bedrooms looking at books and entertaining themselves quietly. As I neared the end of my chore, Kinley came skipping to join me. "We've been playing dentist," she announced, "Look!" And she held out a small white tooth.

Putting together details of that afternoon's game of dentist left me cringing. It was Penn's idea. Sam was his assistant and Kinley got the lucky role of patient. The boys put on their white terry cloth robes, then hurried off to find Dan's toolbox. Choosing their dental equipment carefully, they carried hammer, screwdriver and pliers back into their office, which ordinarily served as Kinley's bedroom.

Settling little sister comfortably on the bed, pillow under her head, Penn ordered, "Open wide." Compliant dodo, she did. Penn selected the tooth that needed attention. A top front tooth, not at all loose, it was easy to get to, at least.

Holding out his hand the way a real doctor would, Penn barked out, "Hammer." Sam complied, slapping the tool into his palm. As gently as he could, Penn tapped on the tooth a few times. He returned the hammer to Sam, then commanded, "Screw driver." Once again, Sam was the faithful assistant. Penn couldn't figure out what to do with that particular tool, so it was returned to Sam virtually unused.

Then came the big moment. "Pliers," called Dr. Penn. He gripped that perfect baby tooth with the jaws of the pliers and began to twist and turn. Big pull. Nothing. More twisting and turning. Huge yank— and out it came! They were thrilled! Neat game! Clutching the prize in her grubby fist, Kinley rushed off to show it to Mom, leaving the dental staff to give each other victorious high-fives in the office.

Appalled, I asked Kinley, "What did you *say* to Penn?" Surely she had told him to stop! "Oh, just '*Unnghh*.' That's all," replied Snaggletooth.

And then it was on to the next adventure.

Aunts, uncles and cousins in Idaho spend much time and energy on water skiing. Whenever we were there on home leave, the kids tried their best to master the sport. Oh, to be like Uncle Tim! He was the resident expert. He went to national competition every year and made skiing look as easy as walking.

Not surprisingly, there came a point during our sojourn in Greece when the kids wanted to work on budding water skiing skills. The problem was, we had no skis, not to mention a boat. Are we discouraged? Heavens, no.

Back in Virginia the previous winter, we bought little toys called ski-boats for each of the kids. They were made of red plastic and were about eighteen inches long. They looked sort of like the lids of shoeboxes, with rounded, turned-up ends, and adjustable straps to fix feet in place. The kids wore them while playing in the snow. Up and down our suburban street, across our lawn, down the little hill into the neighbor's yard. When we packed up to move to Athens, the ski-boats came along.

As the kids settled on their latest bright idea, they dug through the toy box and came up with three pairs of red "water skis." Next, they located a piece of rope, abandoned after the unsuccessful elevator project, and a short handle they unscrewed from the window-washing squeegee. Then, as was their custom, they stacked all their gear by the front door and waited to head out to the beach.

After we arrived there and unloaded the car, the kids raced away to the concession stand where paddleboats were rented. They pooled their coins, counting out the proper number of drachmas, then chose a red paddleboat. It was the one with racing stripes.

They maneuvered it back to Dan and me as we were finishing setting out cooler, chairs and beach mats. The kids were so excited about trying out their skiing idea, we figured we might as well get it over with early on. *Then* we could relax.

All of which is not to say that Dan was truly in favor of their hare-brained scheme. He didn't have high hopes of success. Besides, the beach was full of other people and he figured we'd be in for significant embarrassment. Mom? I didn't care. It was worth a try.

Three suntanned eager beavers threw skis into the paddleboat, tied one end of the rope to the squeegee handle and the other end to one of the cleats at the back of the boat. At last all five us, plus dog, piled in and we pedaled out to slightly deeper water. We reached a point at which the kids could still stand, yet deep enough for them to lean back and float.

The three of them jumped in the water and went into action. Penn chose to be first. Feet in the skis, he grabbed the rope and fastened his grip on the handle. As Sam and Kinley steadied him, he gave the skier's cry: "Hit it!" Dan and I began to pedal as hard as we could.

We pulled him, face first, through the water. No go. The other two got him set up again and once more came the signal, "Hit it!" We repeated the sequence.

By now, a couple of men on the beach saw what we were attempting. Trying to educate us, they strolled to water's edge and yelled, "Oxi!" and waved arms to indicate that we were out of our minds. Obviously, our project was impossible, an exercise in futility. Dan began to mutter. But we tried again. And again.

Dan was ready to throw in the towel, but the other two kids hadn't had a try. We encouraged a change in skier and Kinley took the rope. "Hit it!" she yelled. We pedaled hard enough that the rope pulled out of her hands. We tried again. And again.

At this point, a fair-sized crowd lined the shore, all of them yelling at us. A couple of times we heard something that sounded suspiciously like "Crazy Americans." Dan's muttering picked up in speed and intensity.

Okay. Last kid. Sam grabbed the rope while Penn and Kinley steadied him. Again we responded to "Hit it!" We were tiring, but had to be fair to the third child. We pedaled with a fury. People on the sand continued to wave arms and yell.

What's this? Can it be? It had to be mind over matter. With absolute determination, and using all the strength in his wiry little body, Sam came up out of the water! We pulled him about twenty feet. He was *Skiing!* Cheers erupted from the gallery on shore!

We gave him one more ride, and then headed in. A laughing crowd met us as we stepped onto the sand and we received handshakes and pats on the back from those who, moments before, had (rightfully) questioned our sanity.

As we were on our way to the beach on another summer day, we decided to forego our favorite spot. Instead of playing in the usual calm, shallow water at Schinias Beach, we opted to visit unfamiliar water on the other side of a long finger of land that formed one end of the Bay of Marathon.

Water there was deeper and a darker shade of blue. We even had heard stories of sharks being spotted farther out in the strait, between the shore and the southern tip of the island of Euboea.

We parked the car and began the climb down to a flat spot among the large rocks. Penn and I led the way. Reaching water's edge, we arranged beach mats and stashed our picnic lunch in a pocket of shade. Dad and the other two kids were slow. They stopped to put on sneakers for surer footing among the rocks. Eager to hit the water and cool off, Penn and I donned flippers and masks, grabbed our snorkels and jumped in.

Together we made our way out, thirty or forty feet from shore, checking out the sand and sea plants below us. We always had hopes of discovering an ancient amphora emerging from a centuries-old hiding place, or a school of brilliantly colored fish that would glide near us, just beyond our fingertips. On this day what we saw were ripples on the sand, reflections of sun shining through gently moving water.

The two of us were happy, having a wonderful time in the cool, clear water. I lifted my head to jest with the son who swam about ten feet away. What follows is our entire, actual "conversation."

Mom: "Wouldn't it be scary if we saw a shark?" (idle
    comment)
Penn: "A what?" (simple question)
Mom: "A shark." (simple answer)
Penn: "A shark!" (definitely startled statement)
Mom: "A *shark?*" (definitely alarmed question)
Penn: "*A Shark!*" (terrified answer)
Mom and Penn: "*SHARK!!*" (panicked scream)

We turned the water into a froth of white bubbles as we raced pell mell to the rocks. Dan, Sam and Kinley were doubled over in screaming laughter when we got there. They gave us no sympathy at all for scaring each other silly. As they swam, dived and enjoyed the new site, Penn and I "sunned" ourselves for a long, long time on the smooth, sunny, safe rocks along the shore

◄○►

Sometimes museums can be unbearably boring for kids. Dan and I wanted to take advantage of opportunities to see treasures from the past but we also didn't want miserable, uncooperative kids on our hands. At some point we happened on a strategy that encouraged the kids' real interest.

Whenever we entered a museum we looked for the rack of post cards. Each child selected three cards (naturally, each kid thought his choices were much cooler than the post cards chosen by the other two) and the contest began. Together they roamed the museum, searching out nine specific objects on display. They then decided which item was the best of the choices.

Judgment was theirs alone. Sometimes beauty was the defining factor, sometimes the "best" was bizarre or just funny. It didn't matter. At least they were looking. And, despite themselves, learning. We still have the photo album filled with their dog-eared post cards and, when the now grown kids leaf through it, they remember even the small and infrequently visited sites where the objects are located.

We tried a similar tactic when we visited the islands of Crete and Rhodes. Dan and I each have our own cameras, since we tend to be interested in different subjects. Dan likes buildings and scenery while I like people and color. The kids thought it only fair that they get to take pictures, too.

Dan dug out an old 35mm camera for them to use. We settled on ground rules. Each kid would choose his own subject matter, whatever was really interesting about the things we were seeing. And each would take four pictures before handing the camera on to the next photographer.

Well. That changed things. Rather than chasing around, teasing each other and just generally tagging along with the parents, these three were instant observers of everything around them.

"Will this make a good picture? What if I stand over there? Is it too dark in here, Dad?" They took some fabulous photos. Intricate wrought iron balcony railings, huge old wooden doors with interesting textures, domed roofs of the local monastery. Occasionally a child got an idea for a photo, but someone else had the camera and we walked beyond the location. No problem. We were on vacation. We just turned around and retraced our steps to go back to that spot.

As we walked around the harbor area on Rhodes, we came across the foundations of what had been the Colossus of Rhodes. One of the Seven

Wonders of the Ancient World, the Colossus was a gigantic statue whose legs straddled the entrance to the harbor.

During a cataclysmic earthquake sometime in the distant past, the statue toppled and was never re-erected. But the foundations remained at either side of the harbor mouth. Two tall columns were raised on the foundations, each with a deer on a platform at the top.

When Sam's turn with the camera came, off he raced to the base of one of the columns. He paced, head tilted up, looking, looking for the right angle. Satisfied at last, the eight year old lay down on the concrete foundation and focused on one of the deer. The resulting photo is striking, a magnificent stone animal seeming to float among the puffy clouds.

His turn with the camera wasn't finished, however. We continued to walk along the harbor. Ahead of us were several benches, placed so foot-weary tourists could rest and enjoy the colorful panorama of the port. An old man sat alone on one of the benches. Passing in front of him, we were startled to discover that he was stark naked! Guess he just wanted to take a bit of sun.

Turning our heads, we realized that Sam had the camera aimed directly at the man. Both parents immediately hissed at the budding photographer: "No! That isn't polite!"

Even though it was a losing argument, Sam had his reply ready. "You said we could take pictures of things we think are interesting. And that man is the most interesting thing I've seen since we got here!"

One of our best vacations was a four-day weekend we spent on the island of Kos, only seven miles from the coast of Turkey. Birthplace of Hippocrates, the island boasts the ruins of the "Best of the First" of the hospitals in ancient history, as well as a 2,400 year-old plane tree that the natives claim is the one under which Hippocrates taught. It is also said that the Apostle Paul preached in the shade of the same tree during his visit to the island.

As soon as we arrived on Kos, we rented a car. The only one available, it was *bright* purple. Actually, we couldn't have made a better choice if we'd tried. It was like riding around in a giant Easter egg. Going anywhere in it was like having a party.

After checking into the hotel, we started out on an orientation drive. Where is a good beach? How do we locate the Roman baths and the Greek agora? Where is the castle built by the Crusaders?

We stopped at a promising looking beach, and Dan and I strolled along the water's edge for a few minutes. Working off energy, the kids ran ahead of us. They made their way up a small hill that blocked our view of the connecting beach.

Suddenly, they came to a dead stop. Three kids stared intently at the scene before them. Then, turning around and yelling loud enough to be heard across the water in Turkey, Penn bellowed, "Dad! Hurry! You won't believe it! They're all NAKED!"

We visited the ruins of the hospital, called the Asklepion. Sometimes the kids bought into the theory of "If you've seen one rock, you've seen them all," and this was one of those times. History can be okay, but this place was loaded with huge, spiky horned lizards! We spent the rest of the afternoon there as the kids stalked a succession of ugly reptiles that looked as old as the stony maze through which they crawled.

Another day we discovered a Roman villa where the caretaker encouraged the kids to haul water in a wooden bucket up from the original well in the atrium. Then they sloshed the water over the floor, washing away dust to reveal the vivid colors of the mosaic tiles beneath our feet. Outside, as we returned to our purple chariot, the kids spotted a baby hedgehog in the grass along the path. Examination of the tiny animal consumed another portion of our morning. As I recall, before we went on our way the kids named him "Spike."

At night, we adjourned to the terrace garden on the roof of the hotel. World Cup soccer competition was underway and the TV was tuned to a game between Yugoslavia and Argentina. By now the kids spoke enough Greek to engage in conversation the men gathered around the set. The Greeks supported the European team while the kids cheered on the South Americans. Instant, friendly, noisy rivalry resulted. Traveling with these kids was almost a guarantee of new friendships.

Some time later, we decided we *had* to visit the ruins at Olympia. That trip turned out to be the craziest outing we ever went on. Usually Dan took care of reservations and other arrangements through the embassy travel office, but in the early stages of our planning I read a magazine article about frugal vacations. It insisted that A-class hotels often were over-rated and the B- and C-class establishments could be delightful alternatives.

I decided to save Dan the trouble of making all the arrangements— and save us lots of money, too. Somehow, I came up with a book that listed all the hotels in Greece and began the hunt for a place to stay for one night between Athens and Olympia. I flipped and shuffled through the pages of the book. Zeroing in on economy-class lodging, I spotted one place that sounded terrific.

The write-up included a long list of attractions. The hotel was located directly across the road from the beach and backed up to a sort of lagoon. At the far end of the clear blue lake, caves in the hillside hid natural mineral springs. The site had served as a spa, where citizens came to take the water cure, since ancient times. Photographs showed it to be attractive and inviting.

With arched windows and doors, white stucco walls and red tile roof, the hotel was a graceful building. The grounds featured a network of paths that wound through well-tended gardens. And it was a C-class hotel, a place where we could stay for only twenty dollars a night! Five of us for twenty dollars! What a fabulous discovery! I called immediately and reserved two rooms. A double and a triple, with bath.

So. Off we went. Late in the afternoon we arrived at the hotel to claim our accommodations. Pictures can lie. Likewise, descriptive comments. The place was unbelievable. Yes, it was across the road from the beach, but in between stood a hill covered with impenetrable brambles. The beach was completely inaccessible.

And the hotel itself? Oh, my. It sagged. Everything around it sagged. Even the guests, who shuffled along the tired porch. The photo shown in the book must have been taken many years before, then carefully doctored.

Well, we were there and had no other reservations. We decided we could "do" one night. At the check-in counter in the shadowy lobby, we were met by an elderly woman dressed entirely in black, with an enormous wart in the middle of her forehead and a nervous tic that snapped her head, making her several chins jiggle wildly. She and her ancient wrinkles led us to our rooms. One was a double. The other was … a double.

"Wait. Excuse me. One room is supposed to be a triple," I pleaded.

She looked at me as though I had no sense at all. She shoved one single bed against the other. "Now is triple," she declared. "Three small ones sleep close."

"But we also asked for a bathroom. There isn't one," Dan chimed in.

Sniffing, the woman quickly corrected him. "*Is* bathroom. Down hall. Here."

She opened the door to a large room. Two walls were lined with toilet stalls, each with swinging half-doors. Another had five or six smoky mirrors bolted to its streaked and clammy surface. Below each mirror was an old leaky sink. The remaining wall was occupied by four shower heads drooping from pipes that protruded through peeling paint and dripping, grainy plaster. The drain sat in the middle of the floor.

Dan wasn't just rolling his eyes at me. They were practically whirling.

Usually we were able to make the best of awkward situations. With sighs coming from each of us, we made the effort this time, too. We decided to explore the hotel grounds. The beach might be out of reach but maybe the kids could splash around in the lake.

It turned out to be not quite as clear and blue as advertised. Thick green was more like it. We walked out onto the dock where hotel guests boarded rickety little boats for the ride to the mineral springs in the caves. Sam spotted something in the water. Ah! Maybe there were fish. We all began searching for more signs of fish. Yow! Those are snakes! In moments we counted twenty of them swimming around the dock. This was getting ridiculous.

Now what? We followed one path after another. As we strolled the grounds we encountered only very elderly people. Other than our family, the youngest person around had to be at least eighty years old. Canes, crutches and walkers were the going accessories. By now, the kids had the picture and were starting with their remarks. Like, "Thanks, Mom. Great place!"

Dan's comment sort of said it all. "First time we've vacationed in a geriatrics ward."

Lacking any better idea, we headed back to the hotel. As it was still too early for dinner, we stopped by the car and gathered up some drinks and snacks. A sunny deck lay at the end of the hallway on the second floor, just beyond our rooms. With a table and enough chairs to accommodate the five of us, we claimed the area as ours.

If ever there was a time for a gin and tonic, this was it. Dan mixed two of them as I got out cheese and crackers and the kids opened bags of chips and cookies. Penn pulled three cans of cola out of the cooler. We sat back and visited, enjoying each other's company.

We talked about what we hoped to see when we got to Olympia. We told jokes and even began to think this place wasn't *so* bad, after all. What we didn't realize was that all we had encountered to this point was only the prelude to the main act.

It started out as a kind of drone. We weren't sure where the sound was coming from, but it grew until we all were swiveling our heads up, down and around, looking for the source. We shot curious, questioning glances at each other. The sustained humming intensified, then changed to persistent explosive pops.

Simultaneous recognition came to us. We were unintentional auditory witnesses to a flatulent event that rivaled the rumbles of Mt. St. Helens. A grievously gassy guest, certainly one who had partaken of the sulfuric mineral water cure, was demonstrating a gastric volatility that was positively stunning. On an outside wall, about ten feet from where we sat, a vent led from the communal bathroom and functioned as a wildly efficient amplifier.

Three little faces turned our way. Eyes searched for parental composure. Is laughter permitted? From the corner of my eye, I checked on Dan's reaction. The pain of suppressed hysteria showing on his face did me in. The snort I tried to turn into a clearing of throat was like a signal for the kids.

As they erupted in wild whoops, a propulsive burst of digestive distress, strong enough to launch the space shuttle, was broadcast to the outside world. Unbelievably, a second "voice" chimed in and we were treated to a surreal chorus that left the five of us weak and teary eyed from laughter.

To describe it as excessive flatus does not capture the reality of the situation. Perhaps I'll just say that this was a gastronomical issue of astronomical proportions. Holy elephant! No wonder the mirrors in that room were smoky and the paint peeling from the walls!

We would have been more comfortable *anywhere* else. Like, say, Chernobyl. But, as we already had discovered, there was no place else to go! So, there we sat, as more piteous pilgrims turned the duet into a choir in full cry. It was so extraordinary and improbable that it left us forever immune to the hilarity others find with whoopee cushions at parties. They pale in comparison to the real thing we found at the hotel of Mom's choice on the road to Olympia.

Not surprisingly, dinner in their restaurant that night was the only inedible meal we ever were served at any Greek taverna during our stay in that country. We left there just after five o'clock the next morning. Couldn't get out fast enough.

A couple of days later found us in the parking lot near the ruins of Nestor's Palace at Pylos, beyond Olympia. We arrived there early and the site wouldn't be open for another hour. As Dan wandered beside the fence that enclosed the area, trying to see anything of interest, the kids ran around, stretching their legs and playing some sort of game. Now was as good a time as any for a mid-morning snack. So, I mixed up a jug of Kool Aid and began making peanut butter and jelly sandwiches.

"Hey, kids," I called. "Want some Kool Aid?"

In reply, a deep male voice coming from a spot nearby echoed, "Koool Aaiidd?" Pause. "What kind of Kool Aid?"

Startled, and just a little bit spooked, I nervously answered the voice. "Grape."

Head and shoulders appeared from behind the base of a nearby olive tree. The handsome, smiling young American announced, "I *love* grape Kool Aid."

It turned out that he was a graduate student in archaeology from the University of Washington in Seattle. He was spending the year in Greece doing research and had had no contact with fellow Americans, nor spoken any English, for several months. He simply could not resist making some kind of contact with "home." He was friendly and interesting. And good company. We toured the site with him and learned many details we otherwise wouldn't have known.

It's a small site so it wasn't long before we were ready to turn the car around and begin the drive back toward Athens. The young man was heading in the same direction, going to the port city of Patras. His plan was to take a local bus, but it wasn't due to arrive for another three hours. Enjoying his company, we offered him a ride. It would make the car crowded, but he readily accepted the offer.

We spent a delightful afternoon with him. He regaled us with tales of his time in Greece, of trying to communicate by using the classical Greek he studied in school, rather than modern Greek. We shared American snacks with him, treats we were able to obtain at the U.S. military commissary in Athens. He found Wheat Thins and Oreos particularly appetizing after six months of living on the local market.

Nearing Patras, we decided to look for a hotel for the night. We dropped our new friend at a bus stop where he immediately caught a ride into the city. Dan then drove onto a small coastal road and we soon spotted a beautiful beachfront hotel. It was nice. Really nice. Definitely A-class.

There was no question of returning to our rootin' tootin' rooms at the previous hotel. As Dad went inside to check on the availability of rooms for us, a chorus of "Oh, please. Oh, please. We want to stay here!" came from the back seat.

He emerged, keys in hand, and cheers erupted. Later he confided that, expensive as that hotel was, it was worth every penny. He wasn't about to stay anywhere else. And, averaging the price with what we paid at the other place, we weren't too far over budget.

The CIA Connection

We all remember our arrival in Brussels, Belgium, our fifth overseas post. Following our stay in Greece, we returned to Virginia for two years and then came the new assignment and the excitement started all over again. Once more, we had to prepare to be the new kids on the block. The flight across the Atlantic was hot and crowded and we were late touching down in Paris so we had to hurry to make our connecting flight. But first we needed to locate the cat and dog. Unlike our luggage, they had to be picked up personally and transferred to the departure gate.

Sweaty and wrinkled, we trekked upstairs and downstairs through Charles de Gaulle Airport, looking for the office where we could collect the animals. Precious minutes ticked by before we found the right place. We grabbed the sky cages and set out on a race to our gate. At the other end of the terminal, naturally.

We located the moving sidewalks and away we went, running full tilt, bags and cages banging against knees as we sprinted to the finish line. Leaping off the end of the moving sidewalk, we soared through the air, then landed on solid corridor. Picking ourselves up off the floor, we watched our plane pull away from the gate.

A couple of hours later found us on a train headed from Paris to Brussels and beyond. We had managed to exchange plane tickets for train tickets and there we were in our own compartment.

The kids released the pets from their cages and then scooted the seats out to full-length couches. As soon as exhausted bodies stretched out on the comfy, temporary beds, everyone— including cat and dog, who curled up next to familiar companions— was sound asleep. Except Mom.

Worry wart. I was convinced that if we all went to sleep, we'd snooze our way right through France and Belgium and Holland and wake up in Finland, or something. *Then* what would we do? So, I stood, all the way to Brussels, looking out the windows at the country passing by. I remember almost none of it.

The wheels of the train rolled on, and at last it was obvious we were approaching the capital city. Time to wake everyone. We returned pets to cages and retrieved carry-on bags from overhead storage bins. The train slowed and then stopped. Doors opened and we set foot in Brussels for the very first time. At that moment we had no way of knowing this was a city we all would come to dearly love. It was the beautiful city where the kids spent important growing up years, and they would forever after regard it as "home."

We made our way to the local CIA station and were assigned to a temporary apartment in a building only a hundred yards down the busy avenue.

Early that evening, we began exploring our new surroundings. Just two short blocks beyond our apartment was the King's Park. Only a few square blocks in size, it is nevertheless a welcome oasis of green in the middle of the city. Anchored on one end by the Royal Palace, the park is lovely and we walked through it, heads turning to take in the fountains and statues that adorn the grounds.

At the far edge of the park we crossed the broad Rue Royale and continued down gently sloping streets, aiming toward the tall spire on what we were told was the town hall. We passed clusters of tall, skinny rowhouses with tall, skinny windows backed by lacy curtains, and displaying stones imprinted with construction dates: 1614, 1592, 1635.

As the cobblestone streets got narrower, we turned into a small alley lined with lace and chocolate shops, walked half a block and found the Grand Place. From the first moment, we were enchanted. One of Europe's loveliest town plazas, it is an open square surrounded by elegant structures.

The town hall, begun in 1425, is a riot of arches, columns and statues standing in niches, all beneath the soaring tower. Directly opposite is the fanciful "Maison du Roi," now municipal museum. Filling in the rest of the square are former guild houses decorated with gold painted stone garlands and carvings and bubbled, wavy windowpanes.

Standing in the middle of the Grand Place is like being back in the best part of the Middle Ages. It is glorious, uplifting, inspiring. Most wonderful of all, Dan was being paid to work in this city, where we could visit the Grand Place as often as we wished.

Just then, like an exclamation mark attached to our thrill of discovery, we heard them coming. It was an honest-to-goodness Dixieland band, clad in red and white striped jackets and straw boaters, marching into the square from another nearly hidden alleyway. Our joy turned into a party of hand clapping and foot tapping and just plain feelin' good. Welcome to Belgium!

For a ten year old girl, Brussels is a wonderful place to be, a place where dreams belong. While we stayed in the apartment just down the street from the embassy, the king's palace was only a tantalizing three blocks away. Kinley discovered that the palace was open for visits by the public for one month each summer. Once she learned about the daily tours, she began a nearly daily routine.

Hurrying over to the palace, sometimes with a friend, sometimes alone, she took her place in line. Caught up in her daydreams, she drifted through the rooms and halls. She admired the gilt covered furniture and ornate paintings, turned her head upward to gaze at the elegant crystal chandeliers. Usually the tour was over too soon, so she scurried out the door and rejoined the queue to go through the public rooms once again.

Her interest in the royal family was intense and eventually she learned that King Bouduoin and Queen Fabiola were childless. Ah! What an opportunity! Surely they were longing for their own little princess. She didn't miss a beat. Reasoning that two sons ought to be enough for us, she decided to offer herself up for adoption.

In her spare time, when she wasn't touring the palace or playing kick-ball in the park or walking with Penn and Sam to a nearby french fry stand for a hot afternoon snack, she sat at the dining room table and composed trial letters to the king. It was hard work, finding just the right words to use to sell the royal couple on the idea of why they needed a princess. And why she would be the perfect choice.

When asked if she would miss us if she moved away, she always explained that "when they adopt me, I'll be the princess and I can have anything I want. So I'll ask you to come visit and you can move in and live in the palace with us." But it wasn't to be. That summer passed too quickly and her letters were left unmailed. The royals never knew it, but they missed out on a really good deal.

We all were in such a good mood, just being there in Brussels, that house hunting was anything but a painful chore. Looking around at different properties was like taking short tours around the city and we enjoyed all that we saw. Beyond the city center, the neighborhoods generally featured broad boulevards and there were many lovely parks tucked away to be appreciated throughout the year.

In addition to the tall, narrow town houses and clusters of spacious modern homes, there is still the occasional thatched roof house, and everywhere we went we were impressed by how clean, tidy and affluent it all appeared.

The Belgians themselves are polite, industrious people but they tend to be a dour sort, usually clad in brown, gray and black clothing, rarely heard laughing in public. They do favor good food, though, and their restaurants can compete head-to-head with any Parisian establishment.

Within a few weeks we located a comfortable, roomy house just down the block from a subway stop and up the hill from a modern shopping center. In between was the bakery that became part of our daily life.

Not long after we moved in, I went outside to check the mailbox. There, also retrieving his mail, was the elderly grandfather who lived next door. Hoping to establish a friendly relationship, I started to greet him. However, at that moment my mind went completely blank as I searched for the proper words in French. Frantic to come up with the equivalent of a simple "good morning," I tried to translate from the Spanish "buenos dias."

Buenos ... Oh, that would be Bon. Dias ... I think that's Dieu. So, instead of being content to merely nod and smile at the man, I looked him straight in the eye and said "Bon Dieu."

As soon as the words were out of my mouth, their meaning hit me like a thunderbolt and I turned and fled back into the safety of the house. Rather than the expected and proper "Bon jour," my first comment to that lovely gentleman was "Good God."

From that well situated home, we enrolled the kids in Brussels American School which was about three miles away. One of the smallest of the U.S. Department of Defense Dependents Schools in Europe, BAS was, hands down, the best school our kids ever attended. There were roughly three hundred students in grades kindergarten through twelve, and although the facility lacked fully equipped labs and modern equipment, it boasted a superior, dedicated faculty and exceptionally high academic standards and challenges.

Being in such a small school, all the students knew each other and big kids looked out for little kids. Newcomers were greeted with open arms because every child was needed. Anyone who wanted to participate in tennis, soccer, track, volleyball or gymnastics was encouraged to join the team. Among other activities at the school were drama club, Model United Nations, band and chorus. Academic achievement was part of the whole picture and the kids worked hard to rank high, to belong.

For three happy, glorious years not one of us ever said, "I wish we were somewhere else." For three happy, glorious years Dan and I chased the kids from Belgium to Holland, then to France and to Germany for weekend football, basketball and wrestling.

In that school, extra curricular activities were really special. One year, Kinley's whole class spent two weeks in Switzerland, attending ski-school with several hundred European students their age. Sam's class took part in an Outward Bound program, hiking the mountain trails in the Bavarian Alps along the German-Austrian border. Penn participated in the European Student Art Festival which took him first to The Hague, Holland, and then to London. It was, simply put, a terrific experience for all of us.

Fortunately, Kinley wasn't obsessive in her quest for royal status and was enthusiastic when we moved into the house. At that point she turned her attention to Dad's admonitions to "Be Alert."

Terrorism had become a focus of concern around the world and periodically the embassy issued security bulletins. Dan had discussions with the kids about keeping their eyes open. There was no need to run scared, but every good reason to be aware of one's surroundings, particularly if something or someone seemed out of place.

Kinley's bedroom was on the third floor of our house, a corner room that had windows facing the busy avenue in front as well as down the street toward the shopping center. It wasn't long before she recognized every person and vehicle belonging in the neighborhood. Therefore, any stranger who stopped to rest against a light pole or sat on the low brick wall in front of the house across the street was subject to intense scrutiny by the little watcher.

Even more suspicious to her were unfamiliar cars that parked within a hundred yards of our house. And woe betide anyone who parked and then just *sat* there. If she spotted such a situation, she gave the driver sufficient time to go about his business, say, thirty seconds, and then out came the binoculars.

She stood at the window and focused the lenses on the person in the car, making mental notes about what he looked like and what he was wearing. On occasion, she even jotted down the number on the license plate. Kinley wasn't about to let anything go unnoticed.

One night after dinner I was talking on the telephone with a friend. All of a sudden, Kinley came thundering down the stairs, stopped and looked at me and then raced back up to her room. A minute later she was back, holding a note in her hand. Taught to avoid rudely interrupting anyone in the middle of a conversation, she did the next best thing. She wrote a frantic warning: "A man is breaking into the house across the street!"

Naturally, I ended my conversation and went with Kinley to look out the window. The intruder had made good his entrance into the house and we could see the beams from his flashlight as he moved through the darkened rooms. A quick phone call to the police resulted in his apprehension. Kinley was thrilled! Her alertness had paid off!

At about the same time, the team of communicators for the CIA station decided that our attic was a good location for emergency radio equipment. Our house was tall, it sat on a slight rise and no large buildings were around to block transmissions. In case anything ever happened to communication facilities at the station, the back-up system would be available to keep Headquarters informed about whatever troublesome situation was occurring.

George and Ted were the men who installed the equipment and they came to the house periodically to test it. Sometimes they were at work in the attic when the kids came home from school. The kids weren't aware that the equipment belonged to the CIA. They knew only that it was an emergency radio for Dad's office to communicate with Washington.

Frequently George and Ted stayed on to eat with us after they climbed down the ladder from the attic. The kids enjoyed those evenings because George and Ted were full of fascinating stories. As we sat around after dinner, one talked about a time when he locked himself in the "commo" vault and sent urgent messages back to Headquarters about waves of violence surging through the streets outside, where local victims were being killed by the rioting crowd.

The other told about sitting out a monster typhoon at an Asian post and later finding the basement flooded not only with muddy water, but also with swarms of poisonous snakes.

George related the tale of sharing his office with a dead body in Africa. There, planes flew in and out of the small capital city infrequently and an American citizen died several days before the next scheduled flight. The family wanted the body returned to the States, but the only air-conditioned space where it could be stored temporarily was George's commo unit. The wooden coffin was placed on a bench three feet behind George's workstation. Over the next few days he found it difficult to concentrate on his duties, as creaks from stiffening joints and groans from developing gasses sounded from the box.

The kids listened, fascinated, to the stories. They were agreeable to requests by George and Ted that they not discuss with anyone the radio equipment in our attic. It was neat to be in cahoots with these guys who had "been around." And since George and Ted reinforced Dan's views about security, we knew we could depend on Kinley to continue to scan our neighborhood for anyone or anything out of place.

◄○►

Dan went to Copenhagen to visit the embassy there. While waiting in the lobby for a colleague, he picked up a copy of the diplomatic list for Denmark. Reading through it, he thought he recognized a name.

Back in Brussels, he asked, "Remember Penn's little friend Paul in Chile? The one who had the butler? What was his father's name?"

"John," I replied.

"Look here," Dan grinned, and he handed me the paper he carried home from Copenhagen. Paul's father was listed as New Zealand's ambassador to Denmark.

The next day, responding to Penn's excitement at the prospect of contacting his friend again, I called the local New Zealand embassy to ask for Paul's mailing address. I spoke to a secretary and explained who we were and why we wanted the address for the embassy in Copenhagen.

"Perhaps you aren't aware of it, ma'am," she explained, "but our ambassador here also handles Copenhagen. Excuse me a moment." And she put me on hold.

"What in the world is she talking about?" I thought, as I continued holding the telephone to my ear. Sometimes I'm unbelievably slow on the uptake.

Then I heard a click, followed by a man's voice. "Hallo, hallo!" he said. "Where *are* you?" It was Paul's father!

With delight, I listened as he announced that their family was living just a few blocks from us. He gave me their home telephone number and we made plans to get together soon.

Over the next six months, the boys rode their bicycles between the houses. Although they attended different schools, they got together for movies and watched each other compete in football and rugby. Then Paul's family was transferred to Paris. Their visits became less frequent but, with safe, fast train service between the two cities, Paul returned to spend occasional weekends with us and Penn and Sam traveled to Paris. They had a ball!

Now grown, Paul works at a vineyard in France and Penn visits Europe only occasionally. Nevertheless, they remain in contact.

◄○►

During the summer when we moved away from Brussels, when the kids were growing up and becoming aware of the world beyond our front door, we decided the time had come. Time to tell them about Dad's job and whom he really worked for. We were on our way to a new assignment on the large island of Massena, located directly south of the heel of the Italian boot, and were aware that things might be difficult there, although we didn't know the extent of the problems.

Now that the kids were teenagers, it seemed prudent to let them know the real story. If anything unusual occurred during our stay on Massena, coping would be easier with the CIA connection already established.

We were in the States for a month and Penn spent a few days in Florida visiting friends during the week Dan was involved in consultations at Headquarters. We decided that the easiest way to begin breaking the news was to take Sam and Kinley along when picking Dad up from work, prior to going to the airport to meet Penn's flight from Tampa. Driving onto the Agency compound was sure to spark a spirited conversation.

Within our family, I am known to be "directionally challenged." In other words, I get lost easily. So, as I drove along the Virginia highway with Sam and Kinley in the car, it wasn't unusual when I asked them to keep an eye out for certain road signs. They thought nothing of it when I requested, "Give a yell when you see a sign for the CIA."

Within a couple of miles, one of them sang out, "CIA to the left!" As I slowed and began to turn in to the access road, chatter erupted.

"What are you doing? Where are you going?"

"We're picking up Dad."

"Why here?"

"He works here."

"No, he doesn't. Don't be dumb, Mom. You'll get arrested."

We pulled up at the gate and stopped next to a guard who held a clipboard full of papers. As is required, Dan had left word that we would be arriving, so when I gave my name to the guard, he checked his list and then waved us through. The kids were dumbfounded. Starting the drive along the road through the beautiful grounds full of trees and well-tended bushes, the questions began again.

"Why are we here? What's going on?"

Attempting to be gentle but persuasive, I tried once more. "I'm sorry, but we couldn't tell you until you got older. Dad really does work here. He always has."

Expressions of denial, puzzlement and utter fascination raced in succession across their faces. As we parked in the visitors lot and walked toward the glass doors of the stately white Headquarters building, their questions and comments continued.

"Dad works for the State Department. How can he work here? You're just joking. Right? How can he work for the CIA? These people are spies. Dad isn't a spy. He's an Admin Officer. What are we doing here?"

I tried to answer their questions as we sat on a bench along one wall in the large, impressive lobby, waiting for Dan to join us. Full of nervous energy, though, Sam and Kinley couldn't pass up the opportunity to look around, as long as we were there, and they got to their feet. They examined the huge seal of the Central Intelligence Agency set in the floor, then wandered to the opposite side of the lobby. There they looked at the rows of stars carved into the granite wall. Each star represents a life lost while in the service of the Agency and our country. Unfortunately, there are too many of them.

Soon Kinley was back at my side, inspecting every person who walked by. "Is he a spy? Does she work here? Is that one? What about him?" Her powers of observation already well honed, Kinley was in high gear.

Fortunately, Dan appeared just then. Both Sam and Kinley admit that their father took on a whole new persona at that moment. Even though they weren't entirely convinced he belonged among the spooks, all of a sudden he was a much more interesting person in their eyes.

To this point, Dan and the kids had an ongoing stupid conversation about his job. They asked what he did at work; he explained that he ordered pencils.

"What do you do when you have enough pencils?"

"I order erasers."

"And after that?"

"Then I sharpen the pencils and distribute them."

They almost felt a little sorry for him. He just spent his days doing routine chores while everybody else did the interesting stuff, whatever that might be. But now, out of the blue, there was an outside chance that Dad was actually a man with an exciting life, someone worth knowing even better.

As we walked out of the building, Sam and Kinley bombarded Dan with the same questions they already had asked me. This time he was more straightforward when they asked, "What do you do?"

In the car on the way to the airport, Dan explained that, in fact, he always had worked for the Agency, that his State Department job was only a cover. He agreed to let Sam and Kinley break the big news to Penn, but it could be done only when we were back in the car again. No public discussions could take place, now or ever.

Sam and Kinley were beginning to believe. To them, this was the coolest thing they ever encountered. There was a bit of disappointment that they couldn't tell their friends, yet somehow that made it even cooler.

We met Penn at his gate and he started to tell us about the fun he had in Florida. But Sam and Kinley interrupted, saying, "Hurry up! We have to tell you something in the car!"

Penn assumed they wanted to tell him about Tai, the new Siamese kitten we got while he was gone. But he learned that news over the telephone. That was old news. Words tumbled out of the mouths of brother and sister. "No, that's not it. C'mon, c'mon, c'mon. Let's go!"

In the car at last, the kids exploded.

"Who does Dad work for?" Sam and Kinley demanded.

"The State Department," Penn answered, looking at the other two like they were complete idiots.

And then they were off, on a race to tell him the intriguing, delicious development. Naturally, Penn's reaction and questions echoed the ones we heard before. Half an hour and many words of explanation later, he, too, began to believe.

Throughout the rest of the summer, there were occasional repeated questions at our dinner table. "This isn't a joke, is it? You really *do* work for the CIA?" But the kids only wanted absolute confirmation. They never, then or now, felt any resentment about a lack of openness during their early years. They understood the need for security.

We needn't have worried about damaging their psyches with the revelation. There was no way any of our three kids would suffer emotional harm at being related to the CIA. Like most other foreign service kids, they grew up having high regard for those serving their country. And this was no different, just more secret. All along, they thought their Dad was special. Now, with an extra dimension added, he was even better.

Vlad

The situation might have scared the willies out of anyone. It unfolded during dramatic days that counterbalanced the lighter side of life we usually led.

When we arrived on the island of Massena in mid-July, some of Dan's colleagues in the local CIA station asked if we would consider renting a particular house. Like moonlighting real estate agents, they pointed out all the positive features of the property. They declared it a good house for our family, located as it was in a pleasant neighborhood only a couple of blocks from a main boulevard, putting public transportation and small shops easily at hand.

Not only were there spacious rooms for entertaining, it also had a smashing view. Sitting high on the side of a hill, we could see all the way across the city, right to the sparkling water in the busy harbor. Two patios, each surrounded by clusters of colorful hibiscus and bougainvillea plants along low stone walls, were also attractive selling points. The patio in front, just off the dining room, encouraged frequent dinners under the stars. The other, out back, had a basketball hoop where the kids could challenge each other to one-on-one games.

Another feature made the house appealing— and of particular interest to the case officers. There was an attached, but separate, two-bedroom apartment.

As the case officers explained, they wanted the use of the apartment for a few clandestine meetings with a special agent. With secluded parking available and the entrance to the apartment shielded from the street and nearby homes, it was a perfect "safe house."

They said we should think of it as an extension of our living space. We could turn the living room into a playroom for the kids or use the apartment for guest quarters when visitors came from the States. The case officers' use of the apartment would be limited, they assured us, but in any event we would have plenty of advance notice about any meetings so we could stay well away from the operational activity.

"Well, okay. That doesn't sound too bad," we said. "We'll take it."

It never occurred to me to ask any questions about the agent involved. Knowing something about him might have made a difference in our agreement to live in that house. On the other hand, maybe not. I don't know.

By mid-August, when our household effects arrived by ship, we checked out of the hotel and moved into the house and our life settled into a normal routine. Work, school, shopping, the usual comings and goings of a busy family. But about every six weeks or so, Dan would say, "Let's keep the kids out of the playroom tonight. The guys have something scheduled."

It wasn't long before the meetings became more frequent, however. Now, about once a month Dan would relay plans for another meeting. "Better make sure no friends of the kids visit here tomorrow night. They're coming again."

At this point the kids still didn't know that other people were making occasional use of the apartment. One evening, though, Kinley was late taking out the trash and as she stepped through the door, she caught sight of two men entering the apartment. Dropping the bag of garbage, she quickly ducked back inside, yelling, "Dad! Someone just broke in!"

It was time to do some more explaining. By now, Penn was sixteen, Sam a year younger and Kinley was thirteen and they finally had accepted the fact of their dad's CIA involvement. They also understood the realities of our life and something of international politics. We'd reached the point that they needed to know what was going on.

Dan sat down with them and told them that some case officers were using the apartment. It was a secret and safe place where a man could meet the COs and relay important information to them. He said he trusted the kids to never, ever talk about the meetings to anyone, not even their best friends. Did they promise to live up to his trust in them?

"Yes, sir. Absolutely," the three assured their father.

The white-blond hair of earlier days now turned honey brown, the kids had identical bright blue eyes and their faces were remarkably similar, making it easy for strangers to recognize the family connection. A run of several years of orthodontic treatment on the three had worked its magic and we loved seeing the results as they flashed frequent smiles on their generally good humored journey through their teenage years.

Both boys, tall and lean like Dan, were nearing the six-foot mark and Kinley was keeping a slightly slower pace behind them. Perhaps it was due to the frequent moving we did, when old pals had to be left behind and new friends made and the one constant was their togetherness, but Penn, Sam and Kinley were strongly bonded, not just siblings but loyal friends, as well.

We regarded them as mature and responsible teenagers who could meet high expectations, so we weren't surprised that they kept their promise to Dan. But we also weren't surprised that, taking after their mom, they gave free rein to their curiosity and imaginations and spent hours speculating about the man and the situation involving their playroom.

The clandestine meetings were held yet more often and now occurred about every third week. Notified that the apartment would be off-limits on Tuesday or Wednesday night, the kids knew they couldn't invite pals over to study, to have dinner or to just visit and laugh and listen to their favorite rock music.

Among themselves, they plotted strategies on how to find out something, anything, that was going on. Once we found them standing together, ears pressed to the bottoms of drinking glasses they held against a wall, as a meeting was in progress in the other part of the house.

On the day following a secret meeting, when the kids could return to the playroom, where the television and their games were located, they were especially observant. Their antennae worked overtime and their fervent hope was: "Maybe today we'll find a clue."

And one day they did.

Someone spotted a folded piece of paper peeking out from under a chair. The writing on it was very foreign. Not dummies at all, these three realized that the writing matched the letters on a bottle of vodka they had found earlier in the apartment's refrigerator. Their conclusion was immediate: This guy is a *Russian!*

That night at dinner they happily announced their discovery. I was stunned! I guess I thought the case officers were meeting a local Massenian to gather information related to problems with the host government's economic stability or about labor union unrest within the country. It never occurred to me that we were sitting in the middle of a really big-time spy operation. Even Dan had respected the confidentiality of the project and hadn't pressed the case officers for information. Maybe now he ought to.

Not long afterward, he verified the kids' deduction. The case officers *were* meeting a Russian. The kids were thrilled! Knowing nothing about him, they nevertheless dubbed him "Vlad." Dan got all serious again and reminded them about their promise of secrecy. With a real person now to consider, the kids pledged their silence once more.

Along with school gossip and general family activities, Vlad became one of their favorite topics of conversation at the dinner table. They speculated about his identity and what kind of information he might be passing to the CIA. As happy as they were about the situation, the more apprehensive I became.

These are just kids. What if one of them forgets the promise and tells a friend about Vlad? Will anyone succumb to temptation and, perhaps, brag in history or social studies class about the spies who meet in our house? What if the Russian is followed to a meeting some night? Could possible violence spill over into our lives? Have we put these kids at risk? For me, worries and doubts grew and, at nearly forty years old, I was back to a childhood habit of biting my fingernails.

Worry demands energy and attention; contentment requires little. Over the years, I'd generally been very content, but that wasn't the case now. No question about it- worry took root.

At that point Dan had been working for the Agency for seventeen years, fourteen of which we had spent overseas at various CIA stations. I knew that this sort of situation "never" happens. Home lives of station personnel are kept separate from even the most tedious and run-of-the-mill operational activities. Involving independent wives and children with highly sensitive clandestine pursuits was strictly avoided, not only because of the potential for physically dangerous consequences for the family but also because such involvement violates fundamental security measures meant to protect classified sources and information. Yet here we were.

As the days rolled by, the routine of our lives was punctuated by strange pauses. Whenever a meeting was scheduled, usual activity at the house was subtly altered and we were aware that Vlad was due to arrive. He would stay a while— 15 minutes? an hour?— then silently disappear into the darkness. Wondering if he had already come and gone was like anticipating the rolling wave of thunder that follows the flash of distant lightning. When will it come? How long will it be?

At some point during that time, the case officers realized that we needed a signal mechanism to alert them in case it was unsafe or unwise for the meeting to be held. Perhaps visitors had dropped in, unannounced. Maybe we noticed a strange car parked too long near the house, or a stranger walking too often through the neighborhood, conspicuously out of place.

We settled on a particular outside light. If we ever turned it on, it meant "Stay away!" The signal was intended for Dan, too, as a way to warn him that something wasn't right.

One night he was unusually late coming home from work. Dinner was long since ready and we waited, wondering at the abnormal delay. Finally the phone range and from the other end of the line came his immediate question, "What's wrong?" Penn was the one who answered and he asked in reply, "What do you mean 'What's wrong?'"

"The outside light is on," explained Dad. "I've driven by the house several times. Is there a problem?"

"Whoops," said Penn. "We forgot to turn it off after we put the bikes away. Sorry, Dad. Come on home. Dinner's ready."

The final chapter in the whole episode with Vlad began to unfold on a Thursday, eight months after we moved into the house. On that beautiful spring day, Dan arrived home in the middle of the afternoon. Definitely agitated, he took a deep breath, looked at his feet, then back at me and said, "There are some problems associated with Vlad."

A cold ball of apprehension began to grow in the pit of my stomach. "What do you *mean?*" I asked, with a catch in my voice.

"Well, he is an officer at the Russian embassy. He's a colonel in one of their intelligence organizations and now is under suspicion of working for us," Dan replied. "If he can manage it, he's going to try to get away. He wants to defect to us tonight or tomorrow morning. If it works, he'll come here to the apartment.

"One other thing. He wants to try to convince his wife to defect, too, and bring their two little boys along. Will you help get the beds in the apartment ready for them? They also will need a bit of food in the kitchen."

Suddenly, this was much more than the case officers' earlier talk about using the apartment for a few clandestine meetings with a special agent. We'd slipped into a whole new world. It was scary and dangerous and real.

Of course I would help. This man, perhaps his whole family, was putting complete trust in some Americans to arrange for sanctuary and escape. I wasn't thrilled about the developments, however, and part of my mind was screaming, "Hey! Wait a minute! This wasn't part of our agreement!"

Over the next several hours, as I put clean sheets on beds and hung fresh towels, the house began to fill with people. One by one case offers came, most of them arriving on foot, their cars left who-knew-where, to avoid creating an attention-getting traffic jam in the quiet neighborhood. And the kids came home from school.

Naturally, all the unusual activity piqued their curiosity. "What's going on around here?" they asked.

Dan managed to begin an explanation, "Vlad may be defecting to the U.S."

Just then a very tall, very serious case officer interrupted, holding his hand up in a wait gesture. "Excuse me. Let me talk to them, please."

He asked the kids to sit together on the living room sofa, then pulled up the chair from beside the desk and straddled it backward directly in front of them. Spending a moment weighing what to say he slowly, deliberately began to speak. His voice was just above whisper-level and the kids leaned forward so they wouldn't miss a word. He had their complete attention.

After laying out the basic details, the man then got to the real reason for his little chat. He wanted to impress the kids with the absolute necessity for their cooperation. He wasn't aware of the nickname the kids had bestowed on Vlad, so he merely referred to him as "our man."

"Our man is one of the highest ranking Soviet intelligence officers to have worked for us. The information he has provided is extremely important to our government. Not everyone in our office here even knows about him. Fewer still are aware he is preparing to defect.

"High level defectors are rare and most CIA officers spend their entire careers without being involved in this sort of situation. To have family members involved is virtually unheard of. We are going to have to depend on you to help with our man's safety and escape.

"If he is successful in making his break tonight or tomorrow morning, and arrives here at the house safely, it will be only a matter of hours before the Russians will be looking for him. They're going to be all over this city. They will have all their 'friends' asking questions and listening for rumors about his whereabouts. You must not breathe *one word* about what is going on here.

"You can help us in another way. Please be alert to strangers or unfamiliar cars in the neighborhood. And please keep any of your friends away from the house until this is over.

"It's possible our man will bring his wife and young sons with him. You don't want to do anything to jeopardize two little boys, do you? Are we agreed, then? Can we depend on you?"

There they sat, eyes wide, attention positively riveted on the case officer. Three heads nodded in unison. In effect, they were now part of "the team." They would live up to every expectation.

The case officer returned to the meeting in progress in the apartment and the kids put their heads together, discussing the delicious developments, details and possibilities. This sure beat their usual after school routines!

And Mom? Mom was having a hard day. While I could see and comprehend the whole picture, my main focus was our three kids. Were we putting them in any danger? Were they strong enough, really mature enough to live through this without the pressure getting to them? Were they actually capable of carrying on, as though nothing unusual was going on in their lives? I was starting to be a nervous wreck.

As it happens, coping is a skill all successful foreign service families develop. Those of us who serve abroad for our government learn to deal with a variety of difficult situations. We encounter different languages and customs and often shop in rustic, inadequate markets where available foods are unfamiliar. We endure being away from families and friends and sometimes face frequent interruptions of such basic utilities as water and electricity. We occasionally face extreme natural or weather phenomena and can experience dangerous civil upheaval that results in anarchy.

Since I began my adult life as something other than a typical U.S. housewife, I quickly learned that there were times when coping was required. Usually life went along happily and easily for us. But there were periods when we, like our many overseas colleagues, just did what was required: we got a grip and carried on. Today was another of those days. As hard as it might be, I would try to cope once again.

Obviously, the kids regarded the situation as a marvelous adventure. They actually felt sorry for their friends, who weren't in the middle of something so cool. It was a little hard that day to get them settled back into boring things like homework and, later, as normal a family dinner as we could manage.

Vlad didn't come that night. The next morning, all three kids wanted to skip school but Dad vetoed that idea. Before they trudged down the street to catch the bus, he reminded them of their promise. All it took was a forefinger across his lips. They understood. There also was an unspoken understanding among the three: not one of them had plans for any after-school activity that day. Everyone would catch the early bus home.

Around ten o'clock there was some activity outside. I knew that people had entered the apartment. Soon Dan arrived. He put his arm around me and said, "Vlad is here with his wife and little boys. She's having a hard time dealing with the situation and is quite upset. But, at least, they made it."

There were quiet comings and goings from the apartment throughout the day. Case officers were busy. They called for help from Headquarters in Washington. They needed an expert in disguises. Some were setting up plans for a plane to be brought in which would fly the family to the States two days later. Others were covertly observing the neighborhood, making sure all remained quiet.

When the kids got home from school and learned that Vlad and his family were, indeed, tucked away in the apartment, they set themselves up around one of the tables on the front patio. Nothing going on anywhere in the vicinity of our house would escape their notice.

Soon they spotted their friend Brian walking down the street toward the house. Penn became the decoy, quickly rushing out to meet him and suggesting that they go check out tapes at the nearby record shop. Sam and Kinley stayed behind, serious as could be about their self-appointed guard duty.

If for no other reason than to keep my hands busy and mind occupied, I set up shop in the kitchen and started cooking. Everybody in the house, Americans and Russians alike, had to eat that night so it wasn't long before a couple of baking dishes full of lasagna were bubbling away in the oven. As I tossed salad fixings in two large bowls, Penn, Sam and Kinley appeared. Maybe it was coincidence, but it was at just that moment their often latent volunteer spirit happened to resurface. All three were eager to help carry dinner to those occupying the apartment.

They were mildly disappointed when case officers answered their knocking at the door and they had to hand over the food in the entryway. They never got a chance to walk down the hall to the small kitchen and, perhaps, smile encouragement at the fleeing family. But, it didn't really matter. However small their gestures, just doing anything kept them involved as part of the team.

During the night, a few case officers stayed with our Russian "guests" in the apartment, while others remained outside in the dark throughout the immediate neighborhood, watching to make sure all remained secure. In our part of the house, the kids were restless. They abandoned usual nightly telephone activity with their friends and sprawled on the floor, all gangly-limbed, playing a half-hearted game of Monopoly. It didn't take a rocket scientist to see that what they radiated was a blend of supreme confidence and desperate uncertainty as their attention was focused on listening for any abnormal noise or activity in the area. Although only teenagers, they recognized the serious nature of the situation and as far as they were concerned, the most important thing in their lives just then was the continued safety of Vlad and his family.

If truth be told, Dan and I had trouble concentrating that night, too. As I sat curled up on the sofa, a book in my hands, I continued to read one page over and over again without ever absorbing any of the words.

The next day was a Saturday, so the kids didn't have to go to school. Talk about luck! We were spared the ordeal of an early morning outbreak of imaginary headaches or stomach pains, ploys they surely would have resorted to in an attempt to stay close to the action.

As the hours passed, there was a surreal quality to our immediate little world. It's like everything else stood still. We were acutely aware of the continued discreet comings and goings by case officers and we noted *every* car, bicyclist or pedestrian passing in front of the house. Like deer whose woodland territory is visited by hikers on a cross-country trail, we were suddenly exceedingly conscious of sounds and activity that ordinarily would have gone unnoticed.

At last, the drama played itself out. Late Sunday morning the Russian foursome emerged from the apartment. Vlad appeared first. His hair was now a mass of feathery gray curls and he wore large horn rimmed glasses. He looked like an eccentric genius. Along with his family, also suitably disguised, he was hustled into a car with darkened windows and driven to the airport. Dan was the chauffeur and one of the case officers "rode shotgun."

I remember, vividly, the unease I felt as they drove away. By now the Russians at the embassy were certainly engaged in a full-scale search for their former comrade. Vlad's defection was a serious matter and we had to assume that they would use extreme measures to prevent his flight to the West. Could the family safely escape? What if they were intercepted before they got to the airport? Would all the planning by the case officers be rock solid? What about Dan? Would we see him again?

The ride through the city was uneventful, if somewhat tense. It was quiet in the car. Few words were spoken on the nearly hour-long trip, but eyes moved constantly, looking for any sign of danger.

Finally they arrived and Dan bypassed the terminal, driving right to the plane. Vlad, his wife and sons stepped directly from the car to the stairs of the jet. Vlad himself was last to board. Then, with only one quick backward glance, he was gone.

The kids continued to live up to the trust placed in them and never told the story, even to their closest pals. But they carry the knowledge of their involvement as a sort of badge. For them, it *was* a marvelous adventure. For Dan it was a unique, interesting blip in the course of his career. As for me, even though the experience didn't warp the kids or result in any harm to them, I still quiver when I think of those days.

Subsequent developments and revelations? It's really quite remarkable. Seated around our dining room table, at one house and then another, we wondered about Vlad for almost ten years.

Now we know, for sure. A colonel in Soviet intelligence, he was the KGB resident serving under cover as first secretary at the Russian embassy. He was one of the Soviet agents working for the CIA who was exposed by confessed spy Aldrich H. Ames.

Only a very few of the betrayed agents escaped execution or imprisonment as a result of Ames' treachery. One of these was Vlad. During those days, we were unaware of Aldrich Ames and of the damage he had caused. We learned Vlad's true identity shortly after his defection, but only as the horrifying Ames story came to light did we learn the reason he defected. He was running for his life.

His escape was a close call. Shortly before he appeared at our house, he received a telephone call at his home in the city center. His deputy in the KGB office reported that a message had arrived, directing Vlad to return to Moscow that weekend "for consultations." In fact, Vlad had been identified and was being recalled to face the consequences of furnishing Soviet intelligence to the Americans. But he bolted, just in time.

Our involvement in his escape may have been incidental and limited, but it was highly unusual. It fact, it was unique. Not only were we part of the defection of a Soviet intelligence officer, but the case drew us into the outer ripples of the maelstrom unleashed by Ames.

Vlad, his wife and young sons now live in the United States with new identities. We wish them well.

A Bump in the Road

We hosted a remarkable party during our stay on Massena, on their national Independence Day. It was decided that everyone in the CIA station ought to have the opportunity to enjoy an authentic celebration of the occasion and, somehow, our house was chosen as the site. One of the office drivers, a local man named Andreas, offered to organize the preparations.

Andreas involved his family, wife Sophia and teenage children Alexander and Georgina, in the project. They began their work the week before the scheduled festivities.

The first step was digging the roasting pit. They chose a spot in the far corner of the yard and measured out an area about six feet by ten. Digging commenced and our kids pitched in. This was a unique opportunity. Usually Dad and Mom didn't allow huge holes in the yard. The edges of the pit tapered to a final depth of about three feet. When finished, they lined the edges with softly rounded stones, to help reflect the heat, and filled it with pieces of natural charcoal.

During the week, Andreas and Alexander arrived with the long metal spits. They drove the frames into the ground and checked length, angle and spacing. Ultimately we would have four spits going at once.

On Saturday, major food preparations began. We turned our kitchen over to Andreas and Sophia. First they carried in two large galvanized washtubs—full of fresh lamb livers, hearts, kidneys, sweetbreads, spleens and lungs. Yum. They returned to their car and came back with three buckets full of intestines. It seemed like things were getting a bit out of hand, but what did we know? We left them to it.

Andreas placed a wooden cutting board on the table and began dividing the organs into fist-sized pieces. Sophia, meanwhile, filled the sink with a bucketful of intestines. Taking one in her fingers, she pulled it free and attached an end to the spigot to rinse it clean. This was about the point when Kinley walked in.

Actually, that moment, that whole day, doesn't qualify as one of her all time favorite memories. If we recall correctly, the shiver started at the top of her head, raced through her body and went directly into the floor. She excused herself from the room immediately.

Dan and I offered to help Andreas and Sophia make the kokoretsi, the indispensable side dish traditionally served with roast lamb. But they had their own routine and rhythm and declined our assistance. Just as well, I suppose.

Into the afternoon they worked. They threaded the pieces of organs onto two spits, then wound the intestines over the chunks. In the end, six layers of intestines formed an outer sleeve that held everything together in a single unit. As they finished, they carried the spits outside and rested them on the frames where they could drain through the night.

Andreas and his family arrived early the next morning. By eight o'clock the charcoal in the pit was burning and Andreas and Alexander were fixing two lambs onto spits. The meat was lowered into place on the frames and Sophia and Georgina began turning the spits. Later, in half hour shifts, the rest of us took our turns at the edge of the pit, slowly turning the lambs and kokoretsi.

Shortly after noon others from the station, along with their families, started arriving. Eventually, fifty or sixty people were on hand, with everyone bringing contributions to the meal. Andreas set up three barbecue grills and assigned different men to begin cooking the goat chops. Our epicurean horizons were expanding by the hour.

There was plenty of activity available for guests to join in. Some played volleyball while others had a touch football game going in the little dead-end street that ran beside the house. Eating went on throughout the afternoon and every time we looked, another cast of characters was at the roasting pit, continuing to turn the spits.

For the kids, the highlight of the afternoon came when Andreas explained to Dan that the host is afforded the privilege of eating the first lamb head.

Local tradition, apparently. Did I mention that Dan is a very good sport? He *did it!*

Andreas cracked open one skull and presented half of it to Dan. He started with samples of the meat along the jaw, then moved on to tastes of the tongue … and brain … even the eyeball!

Polite and generous as ever, Dan approached me, holding out his plate. Would I like to share his portion? Well, as it happened, I'd had my go at lunch a little earlier. I was "full." Couldn't eat another bite. No sir. Thanks, anyway.

We've wondered if we could throw a similar party in our back yard here in Northern Virginia. Probably not. It's likely the neighbors would report us to the authorities. So much for establishing a tradition.

Unfortunately, that party is one of the few happy, funny memories we took away from our tour on Massena.

◄○►

Over the years, as we traveled the world, we noticed that our pace was something on the order of two smooth strides followed by a bump in the road. In South America, both Victoria and Quito were fairly easy and benign posts and they preceded the strange dichotomy that was Santiago, a delightful family situation achieved in the midst of political chaos. Joyous tours in Athens and Brussels led up to the stressful quagmire of our assignment on Massena. This tour definitely qualified as a bump in the road.

When we lived in Brussels, the kids were middle school and early high school age and they reveled in the independence they were granted. Using the safe and easy public transportation system of buses and subway, they had the run of the city. With their pals, they went to rock concerts, shopped in the ultra-modern galleries downtown and took in movies.

Our transfer to Massena was not as easy a transition as we hoped it would be. Suddenly we were face to face with palpable anti-American sentiment. Car bombings, often aimed at foreigners, as well as attacks on restaurants and nightspots, were becoming frequent. Now high schoolers, the kids understood the restrictions we placed on their freedom to make their way around the city. They didn't care much for the new limits, but recognized that their very safety was at stake.

Even at school, they endured upheaval and agitation. The international academy they attended had a varied student body and political discord found its way into the classrooms. There were clashes between Iraqi and Iranian students, between Arabs and Israelis, Easterners and Westerners.

Students rearranged desks and chairs, leaving an aisle down the center of the classroom, creating a schism in what should have been a neutral academic setting. Teachers declined to correct the strife-ridden development because they were involved in a struggle of their own.

Despite contracts specifying salaries to be paid in dollars, the Massenian government decreed that the teachers be paid in florins, the local currency, retroactive to an earlier, less favorable exchange rate. Part of the faculty staged teaching slow-downs while others simply quit, only to be replaced by some who weren't entirely fluent in English. It was an intolerable situation and the kids desperately missed their school in Brussels.

During the previous two years, inflation had roared out of control and many private companies had been nationalized. International businesses pulled up stakes and left the country, adding to local economic woes. With funding unavailable for needed maintenance, streets and roads began to fall apart and public utilities suffered. Garbage piled up due to infrequent collection. And resentment began to build among the population. Social unrest became part of daily life.

Security problems and terrorist activities climbed in an upward spiral. All official Americans were being specifically targeted and we had to be constantly alert to the possibility of some sort of attack. Middle Eastern terrorist groups were at the height of their vicious onslaughts throughout the world and it was galling to us to know that local authorities offered sanctuary to them, in the very heart of the city.

We were personally stung by the chaos in that part of the world. Two of our friends had been among those held hostage in Tehran for over a year after the embassy was overrun by Muslim fanatics. Later, we spent a happy evening with Beirut chief of station William F. Buckley in Brussels shortly before terrorists in Lebanon kidnapped him in March, 1984. We prayed for him all during our stay on Massena, but to no avail. He died in captivity.

In what was probably the cruelest blow of all, a few years earlier our good friend Dick Welch, chief of the CIA station in Athens, was murdered by terrorists at his own front gate as he returned home from a Christmas party. He was a terrific man and we miss him still.

We found it impossible to forget the violence that ended his life. We were reminded of it when the American Military Attaché was killed as he drove between his home and the embassy by the same sort of terrorists who assassinated our friend in Athens. And, we remembered when an embassy courier was ambushed as he drove on the busy highway between the city center and the international airport just down the coast. Although wounded, he managed to escape his attackers.

Then the ambassador survived a vicious assault. Terrorists planted a bomb in a drainage pipe under a road he traveled daily. The idea was for the bomb to be detonated by remote control as his car approached the site. As luck would have it, the timing for disaster was interrupted. The driver inexplicably increased his speed just enough to pass over and get beyond the point before the bomb exploded in an enormous roar, shattering the quiet of the morning.

The blast also shattered much of what was left of our feelings of safety and security. It was our choice— in fact, it was our joy— to serve our country abroad. But we were taking a beating from the thundering waves of danger and violence around us. Was it all really worth it? How much more could we stand? How close to home would it come?

Not long after we moved into our house a man came to the front door. He had performed some sort of service for the family who lived there previously, but in an unfortunate oversight, they moved away without paying him. Despite the fact that they were gone, he was there to collect what was due him.

I felt no responsibility to pay someone else's debt but, in any event, I had no money in the house that day. To the worker, however, it made no difference. The other people were foreigners, I was a foreigner, and *he wanted his money!*

I tried to explain to him that it wasn't my bill and I had nothing to give him, then apologized and told him "no." A bully of the highest magnitude, his anger grew with such speed, suffusing his face with a violent crimson flush, I thought he was going to have a nosebleed right on the spot. As I closed the door, he boiled over in a rage. He beat against the door with his fists and roared abusive words about "dirty Americans." Heavier blows followed as he tried to kick the door down. I stood inside, in the hallway, shaking in fear until he finally departed. Frankly, I was terrified and thoroughly unnerved.

Bothered by that experience, by the difficult school situation the kids faced and by the escalating terrorist activities, I began to lose some of my natural optimism about life overseas and the positive feelings about "adventures" we routinely encountered. It got to the point that I hated to leave the house. I didn't want to look around and be reminded of why I was increasingly unhappy.

Then Vlad entered our lives. The accumulated stress finally got to me and I started throwing up before leaving home— and again when returning. Not good.

The awful situation hung like a pall over our heads during those days. Although Dan enjoyed his job, he worried about the affect this difficult tour was having on the rest of the family. The kids longed for the normalcy of our days in Brussels, when they could explore and enjoy the city with their friends without fear. For the first and only time, we found ourselves eager to get away from a post.

In a lucky coincidence, right about then a local newspaper published a story about the possibility of CIA activity on the island. In an attempt to quell the small tempest that erupted, the government declared that an official American would be deported. Rather than have another person interrupt an otherwise satisfactory tour of duty, and considering our own family's sense of turmoil, Dan was willing to offer up himself as the one to go. And so, only a year after arriving, we began planning our departure.

Shortly before we were finally due to leave Massena, TWA 847 was hijacked out of Athens. School was just out for the year and several of the kids' classmates had caught the connecting flight at the Greek airport and were on the plane. We followed news accounts intently as the plane hopscotched its way from one landing spot to another through the Middle East, breathing sighs of relief as hostage passengers were released a few at a time.

Of their friends, only one was still on board when the terrorists murdered twenty three year old Navy diver Robert D. Stethem and dumped his body out of the plane. When the ghastly ordeal was over and the rest of the passengers were safe at last, our kids, too, emerged scarred, having lost more of their childhood innocence.

We were packed up and ready to go by then but because of the hijacking in nearby Greece, the local airport was closed for weeks because international airlines refused to fly in and out of Massena, as well, until its lax security procedures were tightened. Finally, though, we were on the first flight of a U.S. aircraft to leave Massena when the airport reopened. During a layover in

Frankfurt, Germany, we walked to our departure gate down hallways lined by police armed with machine guns and were on the last flight to leave there that day before a bomb threat closed the terminal. The week before, an Air India flight exploded over the North Atlantic, another victim of terrorist activity.

Too much. It all was getting to be just too much. We were immensely relieved when we gently touched down at Dulles International Airport outside of Washington, D.C.

It was good to be home.

South of the Border

"Quid pro quo," George H. W. Bush used to say. We understood what our president meant. This for that. Trade-offs. For the most part, our life overseas was the stuff dreams are made of. Yet we had to pay our dues and live through hardships that came with the territory.

Experiences are relative. Some of the day-to-day problems we encountered would be considered difficult, if not entirely unacceptable, by U.S. standards. However, as we dealt with them overseas they became routine and not at all remarkable.

We focused time and attention on basic utilities— water and electricity— at some posts. There, amoebas, liver flukes and other organisms required us to boil all water we consumed, twenty minutes at a rapid boil. Every morning the kettles went on the stove. We boiled an average of five gallons a day, week in, week out, year in, year out.

We stored it in a big earthenware crock with a spigot near the bottom. The kids learned to use that water, and that water *only*, when they wanted to get a drink. On trips back to the States, when they were small, accepting a cup of water directly from Gramma's faucet was an act of trust and faith on their part.

Back when we lived in Quito, there was a shortage of electricity so a rationing schedule was established. Thursday was the day the lights went out in our part of the city. Since our water was stored in a cistern and pumped from that reservoir into the house, when the electricity was cut off the pump stopped pumping. Tiresome as it was, we did without both lights and running water every Thursday.

For most of the time we lived there, we had a baby in the house. First Sam, then Kinley. It didn't take long to get into the swing of things. Every Wednesday night we made sure enough bottles were filled with milk to last through the next day. They were ready, along with jars of baby food, to go on ice in a cooler. In another cooler we stored juice, cheese, lettuce, mayonnaise and anything else needed for Thursday meals and snacks.

We set aside a new plastic garbage can and filled it with tap water to use for washing up and flushing toilets. And we kept a supply of candles and kerosene on hand. Often, workers at the electric plant forgot to switch us back on at six o'clock. So we cooked on a camping stove and ate by candlelight.

Now we found ourselves in Mexico City, Mexico, our seventh post. We didn't suffer rationing there, but power outages were frequent and completely unpredictable. Some days the electricity went off as many as twenty five times. And we were back to boiling every drop of water that went near our mouths.

But, in an odd way, it didn't really matter. We'd just spent two quiet years in Virginia and while this new assignment took us out of our own country again and followed our difficult experience on Massena, at least we were free from the unusual stresses of that tour and it was almost a relief to deal with the mundane, in the form of boiling water and flickering lights. I really did appreciate the ordinariness of the minor drawbacks because they let me re-group and concentrate on the aspects of discovery that came with exposure to life in yet another country.

Mexico was a delight with its friendly people, vivid colors and rich cultural heritage. Our home was comfortable and the kids were happy, well adjusted youngsters. At this point both Penn and Sam were in college back in the States so we had the pleasure of watching just Kinley as she blossomed in her international bilingual school environment. It was a quiet, content time for all of us.

Despite the emotional beating we had taken during the previous tour, it hadn't ruined our ability to enjoy new adventures and it was important for us to get on with life as we knew it.

◄○►

For sixteen years a sweet natured toy cocker spaniel named Charco (Spanish for "puddle") was part of our family. We got her in Ecuador when she was a puppy, so tiny she fit easily in the palm of Dan's hand. She was blond, with long eyelashes, and looked like Lady, of Disney's Lady and the Tramp.

Whenever we moved, Charco went with us and, being a water-loving spaniel, she relished every chance to share water fun with the kids. In Chile, seeing them splashing together in the pool, she leaped through the air, ears flying, to join them in the water. When we prepared for a trip to the beach in Greece, Charco was the first one in the car.

She took turns with the kids running through the sprinklers in our yards and, later, braved the cold water of the North Sea, nipping and snapping at the frothy edges of dying waves that rolled up onto the wide sandy shoreline.

But whether the day was filled with water fun or not, Charco was always Kinley's best friend. The day came when Penn and Sam went off to school, leaving Kinley at home to amuse herself. It was an almost daily ritual for Kinley to rummage through the doll clothes, searching for school wear for the dog.

Clad in dress, lace-trimmed panties and bonnet, Charco was lugged across the playroom in loving little arms and placed in the child-size wicker chair. There she waited until Kinley filled the other chairs with assorted dolls and stuffed animals. Finally, class began.

Kinley played at being teacher, "reading" books to her students, playing records, singing songs. Through it all, Charco sat in the chair, batting her eyelashes at the little teacher in patient resignation. Classroom instruction lasted until Charco spotted her chance to escape— and then the chase was on.

The dog came running to me, wanting to be freed from her absurd costume, and Kinley followed behind, hoping to return the four-legged truant to their makeshift classroom. Fortunately, Kinley was receptive to the idea of recess! And soon the girl and her dog, now wearing only original silky coat, raced back and forth across the grass.

Years later, as we prepared to move to Mexico City, Dan and I sketched out our travel plans while Charco dozed on the floor near our feet. We planned to drive across the border and take a good look at our neighbor to the south and our discussion centered on what the 2,500-mile trip would be like with teenagers in tow.

The scenario we envisioned was vivid: load up the car and hit the road. Maybe start playing the license plate game. Drive mile after cheerful mile until, after nine or ten cheerful miles, a chorus begins in the back, "How much longer? When will we get there?"

That settled it. We left the kids in Maryland to spend two weeks with Gramma. When we arrived in Mexico City, they would fly down to join us. Our Siamese cat Tai would accompany them but Charco was too old and too fragile to survive the trauma of another long flight. We decided that she would ride with us, snugly comfortable— and uncomplaining— on her blanket in the back seat.

Charco was a wonderful travel companion. She needed frequent rest stops so every two hours we looked for a quiet pullover and lifted her out of the car and attached the leash. Together we walked her and as we stretched our legs we realized that caring for her resulted in a more relaxed trip for us.

At lunchtime we couldn't leave her in a hot car while we ate, so we ordered salads for ourselves and a hamburger for her and located shady areas where we relaxed and ate together. Because of that faithful little animal, we avoided a torturous, pell mell trip.

We enjoyed our drive but, as it turned out, it was Charco's last trip. Mexico City sits at 7,300 feet and that altitude was too much for her little heart. Two months after we arrived there, it gave out and we endured an empty space in our lives.

At the end of that summer, the kids persuaded us that it was time to get a new kitten. Before loading the kids in the car to go off to the local animal shelter, Dan established the conditions for the choice: "No male cat, no long haired cat."

Once at the shelter, Dan and the kids waited while attendants carried several kittens in for inspection. One was scruffy, scrawny and yellow. The fur on its tail wasn't uniform at all. It grew in little clumps, like bristles on a bottle-brush. The tiny animal entered the room hissing and clawing the air. Dan took one look at the feisty, long haired Tom-kitten and said, "That's my cat! We'll take him!" So much for the conditions he set.

They gave a donation to the shelter and carried the kitten home. We named him Fresno. What a bundle of trouble. He climbed curtains and hung from the rods. He got a running start in our bedroom, zoomed down the stairs, flew across the family room, then launched himself through the air toward the large potted palm standing beside the front door. Four legs and twenty claws slashed their way through the fronds. After landing in the living room, he turned and trotted back to our bedroom to try again.

As he got a little older, Fresno discovered a new thrill. Again he sailed down the stairs, across the family room and into the living room. There he jumped onto the wingback chair, bounced against the wall and ricocheted up onto the large wooden beam that ran across the top of the room. Once on the beam, he had the run of all the interconnecting beams of the open ceilings in that part of the house.

Yellow kitten quickly turned into black kitten as he collected years' worth of dust on his fur. This guy was really turning into a pain.

Then he played his trump card. When he heard people come toward the front door, he pussy-footed his way to the beam just above the entry area. A projection there helped keep him out of sight. As soon as they came inside the house and paused, Fresno chose his victim. Seeming to come out of nowhere, he jumped down onto a shoulder, then hit the floor running, leaving the startled guest to wonder what just happened. Which explains why our next chore was rearranging the furniture in the living room.

Our house had the elegant look of a place *House Beautiful* might have featured. It sat on a slight rise with a wide driveway curving upward from the large gate at the street. Off to the left was a big yard with lovely flowerbeds and graceful old trees. To the right of the front door was a pretty little water fountain situated on the stone patio.

Also to the right, set slightly above and gently following the curve of the patio, was the bedroom wing of the house, attached to the main living quarters by a low, wide interior staircase. All of the walls overlooking the garden and patio were floor to ceiling glass. The rest of the walls, both interior and exterior, were brick. It really was very attractive.

It also was in desperate need of some major maintenance work. The roof leaked so bad during one rainy season we had pots, pans, cans and jars under thirty-five separate, serious drips. The main water cistern had an unfixable valve. No one could keep it from getting stuck. That frequently left us with no water in kitchen and bathrooms, but plenty flowing down cement steps out back. Fortunately, the furnace blew up only once.

The bedroom wing backed up to the base of a cliff. In fact the walkway between the house and the cliff was only about four feet wide. Sometimes after a prolonged rain, or during an earthquake, mud, clumps of dirt and rocks of varying sizes crashed onto the roof. It sounded like the Marines had landed.

One morning something else came rolling down the cliff. A baby possum fell out of its nest and landed on the walkway. We were alerted it its plight by the snuffly, screechy sounds its parents made as they valiantly tried to reclaim it. They wanted the baby to climb onto the mother's back, but it was too weak and stunned to accomplish the act.

After more than an hour, the parents departed. We assumed the rescue was successful. But shortly after lunch, Kinley went out onto the walkway and, to her surprise, there was the little possum. It had crawled about twenty feet before collapsing in exhaustion.

Poor little thing. Kinley's heart was touched. We *had* to save it! Well, I can tell you that project made *my* day. How could we possibly save a baby possum, especially one so tiny?

We put it in a shoebox lined with a soft old hand towel. Then into the kitchen where it would be warm and safe. Safe? Fresno appeared and sniffed around like it was snack time. Finally, we got out one of the sky cages and made a nest in a back corner. That was workable. The possum couldn't get out and Fresno couldn't get in.

We called the veterinarian, but he had no clue about what to feed an infant possum. He was interested, but his tone of voice suggested that maybe we had too much spare time on our hands? Oh, well.

We started out with milk, then some banana. And then a bit of canned cat food. The little possum tried all of it. Days went by and we expanded the menu: grapes, tomato, mango, lettuce, melon. The possum ate everything. Remember the old commercial about the kids and the cereal? "Give it to Mikey. Mikey eats everything." It was a natural. Kinley named the possum Mikey.

More days went by and Mikey was starting to grow. We put a small branch in the cage, along with a little ball, so he could run around and play. After about a month, Kinley took Mikey outside for some exercise. She put the cage on the grass, opened the door and coaxed Mikey out. He ran around the grass for a while, but a sound out on the street startled him and he scurried back into his cage.

A sort of routine was established. We fed him— a lot— and gave him exercise. In return, he teased the cat. Fresno sat in front of the cage, beside the cage, on top of the cage, ever alert to the strange little creature inside. Mikey presented himself at the grilled windows and door of the cage and enticed Fresno.

Tail quivering and rump twitching, Fresno launched himself at the cage as Mikey pulled back and stood on his hind legs, teeth chattering in possum laughter. Then he took off on a victory lap around the cage. Up, over and across the branch. Moments later, the two were at it again.

We'd had Mikey for three or four months when we decided it was time to send him on his way. He was a healthy adolescent by now, at least twelve inches from tip of pointy nose to tip of pointy tail. Kinley carried the cage outside and set it beside the woodpile, next to a line of shrubbery that ran along the side of the house. After opening the door of the cage, she returned to the kitchen. Mikey could use the cage as a halfway house or abandon it entirely.

For several weeks we put a smorgasbord of Mikey's favorite fruits and vegetables in the honeycombed spaces of the woodpile. Every morning the snacks were gone. Finally, we removed the cage and left Mikey to his destiny.

In the remaining year of our stay in Mexico, several times we heard bumping sounds against the windows in the family room after dark. Pulling aside the curtain, we saw a possum in the bushes. It looked at us, blinked its beady little eyes, then turned and hurried away. We like to think it was Mikey, coming to say hello.

◄○►

After we left Chile, we were without a maid for twelve years. When we arrived in Mexico City, we weren't surprised when it was strongly recommended that we hire household help with security in mind. Bulletins from the security office constantly reminded staff members never to leave their houses unoccupied. And so we hired Catalina.

It took a while to get used to having Catalina around the house. Yes, indeed. Sweet natured, young and pretty, Catalina was also a hard worker, willing and eager to please. She just wasn't very bright. We never knew what to expect when she was around.

For some reason, she liked to take the curtains down, but couldn't figure out how to put them back up again. We went away for four days once, to visit ancient Indian ruins in the overgrown wilds of the Yucatan Peninsula. When we returned, Catalina set the table for dinner, as usual. Only it wasn't as usual. Everything at each place was switched around.

For a couple of days I said nothing, assuming that she was trying to be creative. Finally, I mentioned that "really, I think I like the table better when it's set the way we used to do it." At that, Catalina confessed. In the four days we'd been gone, she had forgotten how it was supposed to look. That was after a year of doing that daily chore.

At Christmas time, we put a little wooden nativity set on a table in the living room. We arranged it so Mary and Joseph knelt together, looking at the Babe. Opposite them, the three wise men stood with arms outstretched toward the manger. And all around, not really grouped, were the little cows, donkeys and sheep. More or less a traditional arrangement.

Whenever Catalina dusted, she rearranged the nativity set. Baby Jesus lay in front and, placed like a set of toy soldiers, the people kept to a rigid line several inches back. Immediately behind them, the wooden animals were lined up as though ready to charge.

Don't know why, but nobody ever said anything about the nativity set to Catalina. We arranged it, she rearranged it. We grouped them loosely, she lined them up. This continued through two full Christmas seasons. We amused ourselves with the ongoing game. She probably wondered why we never got it right.

These days, Catalina behind us, we still put out the wooden nativity set at Christmas. Occasionally we notice that someone has taken over the chore of rearranging. The figures are lined up again, rigid in their attendant postures and, with smiles, we remember life with Catalina.

◄○►

Our friends Kay and Andy hosted an interesting dinner party when they served with us in Mexico. The guests gathered and cocktails were served. It was a warm, comfortable evening and doors were open so the guests could wander out onto the patio as well as circulate through the living room and dining room area.

Dinner hour arrived and Kay went to the kitchen to ask the cook to carry the roasted turkey into the dining room. As soon as the food was in place, guests would be invited to come to the table.

The cook picked up the platter and started toward the dining room. As she stepped through the doorway, her arm bumped the frame, she lost her grip with one hand and the turkey fell to the floor and skidded along the parquet. A few of the guests witnessed the accident.

Kay was appalled. What could they do? The turkey was their main dish, of course. The quick thinking cook retrieved the turkey, put it back on the platter and said, "Give them more drinks, Senora. And don't worry. I will have dinner on the table very soon."

The cook acted so unworried, so assured, Kay beat back her doubts and returned to her guests.

Within fifteen minutes, Kay noticed the cook carrying food into the dining room. She went to look and there stood a beautiful roast beef, cooked to perfection. The vegetable and other side dishes were not what had been planned to accompany the turkey. It was a totally different meal, but completely done. Dumbfounded, Kay quickly thanked the cook, and then invited the guests to eat. It was a wonderful meal and the evening was saved.

As the guests left the table and the cleanup began, Kay hurried into the kitchen. She had to learn how the cook managed to produce the lovely meal so quickly and effortlessly.

"It was no trouble at all, Senora," explained the cook. "My friend works for the English people next door. I knew they were having a dinner party there tonight so I went to her kitchen and told her what happened. We just traded dinners. We pushed the turkey back into shape and the people over there ate it."

Which reminds me of our favorite dinner party story, one we heard years ago.

The hostess in question was busily planning a dinner party. Since she spoke very little of the language of the country, a great deal of pantomiming went into her communication with the cook. Usually all proceeded smoothly, so there was no hesitation in this instance. She settled on a roasted suckling pig as the entrée.

Wanting the meal to be picture perfect, presentation of the main course was important to the lady. She got out the big tray and acted out her instructions for the cook. "Place the piglet on the tray ... Arrange the potatoes around it just so ... Carry it to the table ... And, oh, yes, put an apple in its mouth, like this ... Thank you."

The evening arrived. Guests were seated at the table. The hostess had seen the roasted pig and it was golden brown and as beautiful as she'd hoped. Time for the cook to make her big entrance. The door from the kitchen opened and into the dining room stepped the cook. Everything was exactly as the lady requested. The only thing was, the cook held the red, ripe apple clenched in her own front teeth.

◄○►

At 7:18 a.m. on September 19, 1985, a crustal plate beneath the ocean, two hundred twenty miles west of Mexico City, snapped as it edged under another plate. A seismic wave, measuring 8.1 on the Richter scale, raced toward the giant city at fifteen thousand miles per hour. Built on an ancient lakebed, which turned into near-liquid consistency with the shaking, the city was devastated by the earthquake. It is estimated that as many as ten thousand people died when homes and buildings crashed down on them.

It was several years later as we were living in that city of twenty million when another terremoto struck with nearly the same intensity. Fortunately, fewer buildings fell, fewer lives were lost. That's because buildings unable to withstand the tortuous vibrations were demolished in the earlier quake. But the terror the cataclysm caused was equally intense because memories were still fresh.

Now sixteen, Kinley was at school when it hit. Although it is an international school, more than half the students were local children who lived through the other big earthquake. Kinley recalls that chaos erupted immediately.

Maps slapped against walls, books and globes fell and desks and chairs crashed to the floor. Frightened children began to scream. Brothers and sisters bolted from classrooms, searching in tears for each other.

In the school office, a special recording was put onto the telephone answering machines after the shaking stopped. The message was that the school was undamaged and all children— repeat, all children— were safe. Over five hundred calls flooded the switchboard in the thirty minutes after the terrible shaking.

At the CIA station, in the city center, Dan was taking a wild ride in his fifth floor office. The building whipped back and forth as waves of powerful energy echoed from first one direction, then another.

The building is designed to be earthquake proof, built on a solid plate meant to keep the structure moving as a unit, so different sections don't strain against each other. And move it did. The shaking lasted over ninety seconds, which is like a lifetime under those conditions.

Meanwhile, at the house, rocks and clods of earth pounded down on the roof from the cliff behind us. As books shot out of shelves and flew into the middle of the floors, I raced between two rooms, trying to slow the wild swinging of several hanging glass lamps. On each trip I just managed to keep them from smashing into brick walls. What an aerobic workout that was! But, I suspect all the heart pounding stemmed from more than just the running.

◄○►

We really missed Penn and Sam while they were away at college so when they joined us for Christmas and summer breaks we were delighted to see them again. And coming "home" for vacation was truly a vacation since there was so much exploring to do in and around Mexico City.

During the week they, along with Kinley and other same-age dependents, worked in offices at the embassy under the summer-hire and internship programs. They also quickly made friends with the young men who were part of the Marine Security Guard detachment and joined their evening and weekend volleyball and softball teams.

At this point both Penn and Sam were big guys, each over six feet tall. They still looked a lot alike and with their short haircuts, they soon heard a repeated comment around the embassy: "Oh, look! Twin Marines!" Perhaps it was their size and resemblance to Marines that led to their helping the CIA station during their second summertime stay with us. On the other hand, it's probably just because they were available.

One of the case officers, an attractive young woman, was working on a project directed against a foreign intelligence organization. Somehow the intelligence service learned of her activity and interest and in a turn-around, they targeted her. They attempted to recruit her to spy for them against the U.S. government. And their overture was made in a particularly threatening manner.

She immediately reported the incident to the chief of station and her tour of duty was abruptly curtailed. For her own safety, she would be hustled out of the country in the next few days, as soon as she finalized reports on her current projects. Meanwhile, she would stay in a hotel and never return to her apartment.

Other case officers determined that the foreign spies had established an observation post in an apartment directly across the street from her third floor unit. To make it seem as though her apartment was still occupied, and decrease the chances that the hostile spooks would try to gain entry for whatever reason, the station needed someone to "house sit" her quarters until a moving company arrived to pack up her belongings, an exercise Dan would oversee.

Since extra bodies were needed to cover the apartment, someone thought to ask Penn and Sam if they would help. For a couple of college kids, this was an interesting element in their thoughts of "What I did during my summer vacation," and they quickly agreed.

Dan accompanied them to the apartment that night and gave specific, detailed instructions: "Do not open the door to anyone but me. When I come, I'll use this knock," he explained as he demonstrated. "Even then, don't open the door until you hear my voice. Keep the curtains drawn and don't stand in front of the windows. Also, do not answer the telephone. You can phone out. Just don't answer. Otherwise, make yourselves at home."

And they did. We weren't worried about them but it was fun to get a laughing call from them later that evening. They were having a great time. Since the case officer wasn't ever returning to her apartment, the food in her refrigerator was up for grabs. They ate sandwiches and all of her chips for dinner. Later, they drank her Coca Cola and snacked on her popcorn while they watched American television beamed by satellite from the States. It was only a small role in a fairly benign undertaking, but they were glad to be given another chance to be a part of the team.

Lt. Wood

Our eighth and last overseas post, Bonn, Germany, was the only place where we lived in an apartment. It was located in a U.S. government-owned housing compound three miles down the Rhine River from the embassy. It was like living in a little self-contained village. There was a small shopping center featuring small versions of a food store, bookshop, post office, dry cleaners, hair salon, gift shop and department store. A small movie theater, an outdoor café and a gas station were nearby, as were the elementary and high schools and a library.

Thirty five apartment buildings were scattered around the campus-like setting, bordered on one end by a huge, beautiful park. Guards controlled access to the compound so it was as safe an environment as we ever encountered in our travels.

One happy result of American communal living was the sound of children's laughter and game playing. In other places less boisterous small fry lived behind fences and we hardly knew they were there.

It was a fabulous place to live and we loved being there. Our third floor, three-bedroom apartment backed up to the park and was only a block and half from the banks of the Rhine. It was a superb location. Except that we had no elevator to help out on grocery days, it was almost heaven.

And as there was virtually no coping required during our stay in Germany, we continue to think that it was a gift to be able to serve there.

There's no doubt about it. Our tour on Massena represented the crescendo in our overseas experience and in Mexico City we began the process of wrapping it all up. The kids started going off to college and took those early steps in becoming independent, productive adults. And Bonn was the starting point of our farewell to foreign service.

Dan and I were on our own as we started that final tour. Both Penn and Sam had graduated from their colleges and Penn was now a young Navy officer serving on a ship based in Guam. Sam remained in Virginia to begin his first job in a project that was helping develop national parks in several countries around the world and Kinley was in her senior year of college.

Every time we lived in the States I worked at the little local newspaper. I did it mostly for fun but in recent years we needed the extra income to help pay for schooling costs. Now, though, with only two semesters of college tuition to go and so much to see and do there in Europe, my "job" became that of travel director for our weekend jaunts around the area. I pored over our collection of maps and travel books, locating small picturesque towns, castles, even little known remnants of long-ago Roman occupation, and then away we'd go, exploring the countryside and meeting the people who live there.

One small town we got to know was the charming old village of Weinheim, near Heidelberg, where Dan's ancestors lived during the 1700s. It is full of quaint and cozy pastel painted cottages and tall, steep-roofed buildings with exposed beams and colorful flower boxes hanging from window sills, located along tiny, windy cobblestone streets and is still surrounded by the heavy stone walls that defined and defended the original small settlement.

Bonn is well situated, with access to several major autobahns, so it was easy to take day trips into Holland, Belgium, Luxembourg and France. We visited all these places and got into a routine of returning to Brussels about every six weeks or so to visit old friends and favorite haunts there. It really seemed to be a classic case of "so much to see and do, so little time." We were out and about so often that we now look back and realize that we spent only about a dozen full weekends in town during a two-year span.

Over the years we attended lots of parties and gatherings and celebrations. In truth, they now blend together, if they aren't entirely forgotten. One event to which we were invited and certainly remember, occurred one weekend evening when were at home in Bonn. The movie "Schindler's List," produced and directed by Steven Spielberg, was opening with special showings in several locations throughout Germany.

A number of invitations were made available to the official American community. We were happy to receive tickets for the showing since we have a continuing interest in the history of World War II and were already familiar with the story of Oskar Schindler. We also knew the movie was opening to critical acclaim around the world and we wanted to see it.

Representatives of the German government and officers of branches of the German military attended the showing, as did members of the staff of the Israeli embassy located in the German capital. As we arrived we felt there was something special about viewing the movie in the company of an audience made up primarily of Germans and Jews.

In fact, nothing *happened*. But the atmosphere in the theater was so intense, with the viewers able to relate to that time in history on such a personal level, that it touched us deeply. There was sorrow and shame and regret so palpable that there could be no doubt as to the reality of the Holocaust. Had we viewed the movie back in Virginia, it would have moved and impressed us, but seeing it there, in the midst of people who were personally affected by the reality of it all, on both sides, was a remarkable experience.

At the end of the movie, there was no movement. There was utter silence. The audience sat in intensely reverential tribute to the victims and to the power of the movie. Finally, as we made our way into the lobby and out onto the street, we observed a touching encounter between two men. They stopped and looked into each other's eyes. The German gentleman quietly said, "I am so very sorry," nodded his head briefly at the Jewish man, and then they parted.

Acknowledgement, healing, hope. We were privileged to witness such a moment.

—◦—

As we enjoyed ourselves there in Bonn, Kinley's days in college began to wind down. It was one of those years when jobs were hard to come by for new graduates and as Kinley dipped her toes in the pool of possible employment, her initial probes were chilly and discouraging. The weeks sped by with no positive developments and we recognized that our daughter was going to need significant support, for the basics of rent, car and food, for an indefinite period.

So, in a telephone conversation just a few weeks before graduation, Dan tried to reassure Kinley that we wouldn't let her sink. "Now listen, sweetie. Consider this: if you simply cannot find a job, maybe you'd come over here. You could get a small job, perhaps in the embassy or at one of the schools, and it would be a whole lot less expensive if you'd stay here with us. Will you think about it?"

"Oh, thanks, Dad. I really appreciate the offer, but I don't know," Kinley replied. "There are still a few more places I want to apply. But I'll let you know." And the conversation ended.

On her end, though, (as we were to learn from her some time later) she hung up the phone, spun around, threw her arms in the air and squealed in delight to her roommates, "I'm going to Germany! I'm going to Germany!"

And so our happy, funny, youngest child joined us for our final year in Europe. She did get a job at the embassy, in fact, and quickly made friends with a large group of other young adults in the international community. She added another element of joy to our time in Bonn and we thoroughly enjoyed her company.

Not long after her arrival, my cousin Susan and her husband Ralph came to visit us. We were their home base as they took several trips on their own in a rented car. One of their trips was to the Alps area of southern Germany, Switzerland and Austria.

They scheduled only a few days for that particular outing. But Ralph is a racecar driver. On the wide-open autobahns, he let 'er fly. Like many men, once underway he resisted requests from the passenger seat to stop. We laughed at the mental image of the two of them speeding through Europe, Ralph gripping the steering wheel with intensity as Susan aimed her camera out the window at glorious scenes passing in a blur.

They did stop long enough to tour one of the wonderful castles in Bavaria, Neuschwanstein, Mad King Ludwig's masterpiece. At the bottom of the hill from the fairy tale castle, they waited in line to catch a bus for a ride up to the base of the castle.

Even though they spoke no German, they were coping well with all they encountered on their adventure. Still, Susan was interested when she *thought* she heard two women ahead of them in the line say something in English. If she and Ralph needed any assistance or information, perhaps the women could be of help.

Susan kept her eye on the ladies and when they boarded the bus, she chose a seat near them. Although reluctant to intrude on their privacy, she finally attempted to communicate with them. As slowly and distinctly as possible, and slightly louder than necessary— as though those who speak another language are also hard of hearing— she articulated her question.

"Wwhheerree – aarree – yyooouu – ffrrroomm ?"

One of the women was pleased to be able to respond to Susan's conversation opener. With a friendly smile on her face, and as slowly and distinctly as Susan had spoken, she answered. "Cchhii – ccaa – ggooo."

After Susan and Ralph left, we returned to Virginia for a ten-day visit and a happy family reunion. Then it was back to Bonn where we had only twenty-four hours to prepare for some more visitors from the States. It was a whirl-wind of shopping for food, cleaning the apartment, checking in with friends and colleagues. Then the guests arrived.

Ignoring jet lag, we hit the road. We took them to see quaint, colorful villages and wonderful medieval castles. They enjoyed cruises on both the Rhine and Mosel Rivers. We went through Holland on our way to Belgium, and we visited the remains of the bridge at Remagen, Germany, where the Allies crossed the Rhine during World War II.

Finally, I *had* to stop and take care of some housework, including piles of accumulated laundry. No problem. Our guests could take the train by themselves to Cologne, visit the immense cathedral there, see the sights and return in time for dinner. So, in went the clothes. Washer, dryer. Next load. And the next.

What we didn't know was that while we were gone, some birds got into the dryer vent tube. Running from the laundry area to the stuck-open hinge on the outside of the building the tube was about ten feet long. After the first bird got in, he invited his closest friends to join him. As the tube became more crowded, newcomers pushed original settlers to the back. One by one, they fell down the extension vent leading directly from the dryer. They couldn't get out and they died.

No, I didn't smell anything. Of course, we hadn't spent much time in the apartment. And while doing laundry, I was also running around changing sheets and towels, dusting and vacuuming. Meanwhile, the heat from the dryer was doing its work.

As I stooped to open the door of the dryer, I noticed lint on the floor. Actually, on closer inspection, it looked like someone had spilled extra-long grained rice everywhere. What *is* that? When I touched a piece to pick it up, it wiggled! *Yecchh!* Maggots! Swarms of soft-bodied, legless larvae from hell were emerging from under the dryer.

That may be the all-time fastest I ever made it to the telephone. Calling the maintenance unit, my voice conveyed definite urgency as I requested immediate assistance. As luck would have it, Dan— clever man— had left for Berlin that morning for a three-day trip. He missed all the fun.

By the time the maintenance crew arrived, the laundry area was pulsating with the disgusting invaders. The men removed the dryer, then the extension vent. They brought in an air compressor and blew out the long main tube. Altogether there were nine dead birds. As they put a new, bird-proof vent on the exterior and replaced the old dryer with a new one, I began the interior clean up.

Two mop jobs, two Clorox rinses. At last I was satisfied it was clean enough to live with. The next day was laundry day again. Re-washing those loads just made me feel better. Then we forgot about the episode as best we could and life went on.

Those guests finished their stay with us and departed, followed three days later by the next round of visitors. Again, we hit the road. On Saturday morning we decided to take a picnic lunch and head out to see some sights.

I opened the door to the laundry area to get the cooler— and out swarmed the flies. Huge, black flies. Hundreds of them. It was like an invasion out of "The Birds." Resembling juicy black olives with wings, and in formation like squadrons of bombers on saturation runs, they droned their way into every room in the apartment.

It wasn't a new infestation. Just the remains and results of the previous mess. Unseen, great bunches of the maggots had crawled up onto the inner framing of the washer. We never thought about that possibility. There they stayed, cozy and protected and maturing the whole time. And they all "bloomed" at once.

As it happened, we had acquired a small collection of fly swatters as gag gifts. There they were, a zapper-gun model, little hands, little feet, even one that screams when it lands a blow. Each of us, family and guest alike, grabbed a swatter and the hunt began. During a surreal, disgusting, but nevertheless funny half-hour, we stalked them mercilessly - Slap! Whack! Swat! - then swept up the remains and finally headed out the door to continue our exploring.

The only time in our overseas life that we experienced flooding was during that tour in Germany when the Rhine River surged over its banks. We watched with concern as the river rose, and felt an eerie fascination as an attractive restaurant directly across the river from us was consumed. Water inched up, covering windows and doors on the ground level. Next, the second floor disappeared from sight and finally we could see only the tip of the weather vane attached to the roof.

Meanwhile, flooded storm drains in our compound couldn't carry any more run-off and the water backed up. Seepage from the ground itself took on a life of its own. Just before water started pouring into our basement, Dan, Kinley and I, along with other families in the building, worked for hours carrying storage items upstairs. What we couldn't move, we stacked as high as we could.

Oddly, some people stayed in their apartments and watched television. Later, they were the ones who complained— about the mud and mess and wet belongings.

The maintenance unit brought pumps and hoses to us. As we pumped the water out, it added to the flood in the front yard. Then we watched most of it find its way back into the basement.

At one point, two local workmen appeared. Perhaps they worked for the city. They decided that a heavy drain cover in the basement floor led to a usable storm drain. They pried it open but, unfortunately, it wasn't a storm drain. Just our luck, it was the main sewer line and, given an outlet, raw sewage gushed into the basement, adding to our mess. The two "helpers" departed, never to be seen again.

◄o►

Our last adventure in our overseas experience was one of the best. Dan and I read the book, "*A Time for Trumpets*," by Charles B. MacDonald, a chronicle of the Battle of the Bulge. We were interested in it not only because of the history but also because we love the Ardennes region of Belgium, where the action occurred. We were familiar with many of the towns and villages involved. One story in the book really caught our imaginations.

During the fighting in mid-December, 1944, hundreds of GIs were caught behind shifting German lines in the vicinity of St. Vith, Belgium. Lacking maps and compasses, many of the soldiers managed to elude the enemy and make their way back to American positions. Less fortunate ones blundered into German-held pockets and were taken prisoner. Others were killed when they were spotted in their race to escape.

Among those who sprinted from hiding spots in the hedgerows to protective cover among the trees, was a young American, Lt. Eric Fischer Wood.

According to the book, Lt. Wood made his way to within three miles of American lines but then, inexplicably, decided to remain in the forested area just outside the village of Meyerode. Reports by Belgians who survived the surge of battle suggest that a small number of other American stragglers banded together with Lt. Wood in the forest. There, over the next weeks, they waged a small-scale guerrilla war against the Germans.

They harassed the Nazi troops, attacking their supply dumps and columns, ambushing them whenever possible. Residents of the area heard small arms fire coming from the forest and observed wounded Germans stumbling into their town, complaining about a band of still-fighting Americans roaming the woods.

When the tide of the armies swept beyond the region, Belgians went into the forest where they found the body of a big, young American officer with the bars of a lieutenant on his uniform. The bodies of seven German soldiers surrounded him.

The U.S. Army listed Lt. Eric Wood as having been killed in action on December 17, 1944. His father, a Brigadier General on Eisenhower's staff, learned of the valiant fight by the young lieutenant near Meyerode and felt certain it was his son. He had no doubt that Eric Wood lived beyond December 17, dying some weeks later in that Belgian forest.

In an effort to document the incident, and ultimately have his son honored with a posthumous Medal of Honor, General Wood collected affidavits from residents of the area. He pieced together an intriguing story, but it was not definite enough to persuade U.S. officials to change their earlier declaration.

The Belgians were convinced, however. They were certain about Lt. Wood's valor. Determined to recognize his sacrifice, they erected a monument in his name. The book describes the monument: "Set at the edge of a patch of fir trees along an almost eerily silent gravel trail, it is a touching memorial."

It was a tantalizing clue. If ever we had stumbled on a fascinating challenge, this was it. Could we find the monument, knowing only "Meyerode … forest … gravel trail?" We decided it was enough for us.

On the next Saturday, Dan and I hopped in the car and headed toward the Ardennes. We took a dog-eared road map of the area around St. Vith. Unfortunately, it didn't show the village of Meyerode. We also carried the book we were reading, since it had a map of the World War II battle lines, complete with lines and arrows and jagged arcs that look like teeth marks. At least the battle map showed Meyerode.

When we arrived in the St. Vith area, we realized that we had a bit of a problem. Belgium is a bilingual country, reflecting French and Flemish communities within its borders. Road signs list names of towns and villages in both languages. Often the spellings and pronunciations vary wildly and the directional arrows read Antwerpen/Anvers, Liege/Luik and Ambleve/Amal.

On our visit that day, we witnessed the results of a recent outbreak of partisan rivalries. Vandals armed with cans of spray paint roamed the area and obliterated many of the names of towns and villages from directional signs along the roads. French names of towns were painted over in blue. Red paint covered the Flemish names. We were left to navigate our way to Meyerode with only the two maps we carried.

We parked beside a bakery in St. Vith and bought fresh croissants. Then, sitting in the car and dropping flaking crumbs on laps and maps, we looked from one page to the other, trying to reconcile the two. "Well," we decided, "Let's get moving. We'll just explore whatever paths we come to."

We drove out of St. Vith, east, then north, and ended up in Schoenberg. We tried again and came to Herresbach. How hard can it be to find a town?

It was a crazy afternoon. We zinged off on one wrong road after another. At one point we found a sign, a wooden arrow that read, "Meyerode, 7 km." Feeling victory within our reach, we laughed and followed its direction. At the 7 km. point, we spotted another wooden arrow that taunted us: "Meyerode, 9 km." We ended up in Ambleve.

Well into our search, even now we have no idea where we were, we saw a group of people gathered outside an old brick house. Perhaps they could tell us how to get to Meyerode. For some perverse reason, Dan decided I should practice my long-forgotten French and he insisted that I be the one to do the asking. Reluctantly, I got out of the car and approached the five old men and one old woman.

I held out the book with the old battle map, pointed to "Meyerode" and asked, slowly and distinctly— in English— "How can we get to Meyerode from here?"

They looked at me in stunned silence. I reached into my rusty memory bank and, at last, came up with a question in French, "Ou est Meyerode, s'il vous plaît?"

I might as well have stepped out of my space ship and made beeping sounds at them. They seemed to not understand a single word. Ever more slowly and more distinctly, I asked my question in French once again, tapping the map repeatedly with a fingertip for emphasis. Suddenly the six elderly people responded simultaneously.

I have *no* idea what they said. But they *did* understand the gist of the question and they did want to be of help. They conferred among themselves, then looked at me and, again speaking at the same time, they each pointed in a different direction.

We looked at each other blankly and they tried again. One man took the book and pointed at Meyerode. We all nodded our heads. Another man produced a pencil and drew an arrow on the map and wrote, "Ambleve."

A third man pretended to drive a car. Hands and arms rocking back and forth in front of him, he walked a few paces, turned right, went a few more steps and turned left. "Voila!" he said. "Meyerode!"

The woman joined in the conversation. "Non, non, non!" she exclaimed. She pointed with conviction in the opposite direction.

As I began to conclude that these people hadn't the foggiest idea how to get to Meyerode, I realized that they had touched me. Literally. Every single one of them had found an opportunity to touch me. Gently, on the shoulder or on my arm, each one reached out and touched this foreigner. All of a sudden, the thought came that they might not have seen an American since the long ago war raged in their back yard.

Although they weren't able to assist, they really had tried. I smiled at them and thanked them. One of the men said, "Ah, non, Madame. Merci, America." Dan and I still were no closer to our destination but that short stop along the road was a delight.

An hour later, after more wandering, we found ourselves in the village of Wallerode. This was real progress. The battle map showed Meyerode only three miles away. Unfortunately we sat at a spot where the road branched into three small lanes, each heading more or less northward. Which one to take? Another car was pulled over at the side of the road and the four passengers were discussing something and gesturing at the roads.

Dan stepped out of the car and spoke to the other driver. "Excuse me. Could you help us?"

To which the man replied, "Ah. Americans. How may I help you?"

"Do you know which of these roads leads to Meyerode?" Dan asked.

The man laughed and replied, "Are you going there, too? We've been looking for it for hours! We are supposed to join a volksmarch there."

Just then a woman came out of a nearby house and began to gather clothes hanging from a line in her yard. The other driver got out of his car and approached the woman, asking for directions. She immediately pointed at the lane to the right, the narrow one that led between low stone walls. Looking like a long private driveway, it had seemed our least likely choice. But the friendly Belgian returned to his car and cheerily called to us, "Follow me!"

In tandem, and within minutes, we finally arrived in Meyerode. Now what? The village was surrounded on three sides by heavy, lush forests. How would we ever find the monument to Lt. Wood?

We parked beside our new friends from Antwerp, next to the graceful old stone church in the middle of the village. They were too late to join the organized walk but had decided to stroll other paths on their own. Before they left, they accompanied us when we spotted an old woman placing flowers in the nearby cemetery. Perhaps she knew where the monument was located.

Indeed, she did. She had seen it many times, she said, when she walked through the forest. "How can we find it?" we asked.

Well, she couldn't explain exactly, "But it is in *that* part of the forest, right over there." And she pointed a trembling hand back across the village and up the gentle rise of a hill. "Look there. Go down the trails. You'll find it."

We thanked the people who had assisted us and drove back through the village toward the wooded hillside. At a curve in the road, a hard packed dirt lane ran alongside an old stone barn. Next to a large tree by the barn stood a wooden pole with several directional arrows nailed to it.

Go this way to Wallerode, that way to Ambleve, they directed. One arrow contained the information we sought. It read, "E. Fischer W. U.S. monument, 1200 meters." And it pointed up the lane.

Interesting that the Belgians chose to emphasize Lt. Eric F. Wood, Jr.'s middle name on the sign. But we didn't care. We were almost there.

We calculated how many meters equal how many tenths of miles and we watched the odometer as the car climbed the hill, into the shadows of the trees. At precisely 1200 meters, we stopped.

We had reached an intersection in the woods and *six* logging trails led away in different directions! At this point, what else should we have expected?

We parked the car and began walking through the woods in ever widening circles. We didn't know what the memorial looked like so we weren't sure exactly what we were hunting for. In half an hour of looking, the only thing that caught our attention was a clump of the most beautiful mushrooms we had ever seen. Bright red and decorated with white polka dots, they were a foot tall. The caps were as big as dinner plates.

What a perfect thing to find in a European forest! If Hansel and Gretel didn't live nearby, surely little gnomes were observing us from the safety of thickets around us.

We were enchanted, but by now it was getting dark in the forest. Soon we would have to get back on the road toward Bonn. We decided to drive a short way down each of the logging trails. We saw pretty glades, extravagant growths of ferns and handsome stands of pine trees and hardwoods. But no monument.

Obviously a monument existed and we knew we were close to it. We would try again. Next time we wouldn't have to drive on every back road, lane and trail in the Ardennes. Next time we could come directly to Meyerode and have all the time we needed in the woods to locate the memorial.

So, at a wide spot in the trail we turned around. We made our way back to the intersection in the woods, where the six logging trails joined. Just then we saw a young Belgian man, his wife and two little girls sitting on fallen logs, resting after a walk through the forest. Maybe they knew where we could find it.

Actually, they didn't. But the young man had listened to his parents and neighbors tell stories about the war. Surely they knew about Lt. Wood. If Dan cared to telephone him next week, he would find out what he could. Leaving it at that, we returned to Bonn.

Over the next several days we told our friends the story of Eric Wood and about the difficulties we had finding the village of Meyerode. Everyone was intrigued and many mentioned that they, too, would like to visit the monument. And so the idea of a "rally" took root.

Wouldn't it be fun to get a bunch together, provide each car with the same maps we used, and meet at the church in Meyerode? Then we could go into the forest to search for the monument together. Later, we could have a picnic.

We made copies of the maps and drew up emergency directions, which we put into sealed envelopes. If anyone was still lost at eleven o'clock on the morning of the rally, they could open the envelope and have easy-to-follow directions to the village. The group would wait at the church until noon for any stragglers.

Dan telephoned the young man in Meyerode. His name was Pavel and he had directions to the monument ready for us. As it turned out, had we continued on down one of the trails just a little farther, we would have found it. It was only about fifty feet beyond the gentle curve where we turned the car around.

Pavel's inquiries had sparked conversations among residents of Meyerode. Those who had been there during the war remembered the stories about the small band of American soldiers roaming the woods and attacking the Germans. They told Pavel another story centered on a farmhouse down the road from the monument.

During the time Lt. Wood hid in the forests, the Germans took over the farmhouse to use as a temporary headquarters. As battles raged through the area, German soldiers captured American equipment, including jeeps. Like Wood, other GIs caught behind the lines were moving furtively through enemy territory in a desperate attempt to rejoin their own forces.

One night two U.S. jeeps were parked in the farmyard not far from the house. Quietly, carefully, the jeeps were reappropriated. They were pushed out to the road and then used by GIs in a mad race back to the relative safety of American lines. Residents of Meyerode remember irritated complaints made later by some of the Nazi troops who were in the farmhouse at the time.

We set the rally for a Saturday morning in April. Altogether we were twenty people in eight cars. Eighteen adults, two children and one very large dog. All of us were part of the official U.S. community in Bonn and we were sincere about wanting to salute the gallantry of fellow Americans who fought under our country's flag nearly fifty years before.

We met in the parking lot near the little movie theater in the housing compound. We handed out the maps and synchronized our watches. Then we were off.

Surprisingly, to us anyway, all cars but one were parked at the church by eleven o'clock. Obviously most of our friends were better navigators than we had been. Last to arrive, an hour later, were Tom, Christa and their dog Seamus. Like us, they had seen much of the local countryside.

As we waited for them, April in the Ardennes had a surprise for us. Clouds moved in and we were caught in a real snowstorm. So much for our planned picnic in the woods. It didn't dampen our spirits, however. We drove into the forest and, with the help of Pavel's directions, found the monument in a very short time.

It is a stone cross about five feet high, just off the narrow gravel road. All around are hardwood trees, growing straight and tall. Setting off the memorial is a stand of pine trees planted in a graceful arc about fifteen feet behind the cross.

In the fall, when the leaves of the hardwood trees shimmer in golden beauty, a green curtain of pine boughs frames the monument. Anyone who passes by knows the memorial stands in recognition of something special.

We carried along a bouquet of fresh flowers to lay at the foot of the monument. And so we did, with soft snowflakes falling onto the petals. We were touched to see that local residents continue to come to pay their respects. On one side of the monument was a still living, simply decorated Christmas tree, planted in a plastic bucket. On the other were the remains of a dried arrangement of autumn flowers. The handful of Americans who found our way there appreciate the devotion of Belgian caretakers who remember.

It was a wonderful adventure to have in the final months of our overseas service. We couldn't have planned a better one.

◄○►

Somehow, it came suddenly, like the slam of a door. It was the day the packers arrived at our apartment in Bonn. That eighth and final tour was drawing to a close. Time to wrap it all up and return home. In truth, we weren't entirely ready. What a life we had led! We wouldn't trade it for anything. Our overseas experience was unbelievably special and saying goodbye to it was something of a jolt.

In fact, we discussed the possibility of accepting one more assignment, but then considered the pattern we had already set— those two smooth strides followed by a bump in the road. Had our rhythm held, on any tour following

Mexico City and Bonn, all hell probably would have broken loose. Why push our luck? We decided we could do without further "excitement" and hardships. Eight tours was plenty. So, with more living to do and lots of things out there to discover and experience, we made another big move, from Germany back to the USA.

Leaving Bonn, we went to England where we visited with Frank and Margaret, our good friends from days in Victoria. Then, in a dream come true, we boarded the Queen Elizabeth II for the trip across the Atlantic. And we really experienced the Atlantic. It was one storm after another, with waves breaking high over the bow.

Since we were on the budget plan, ours was a closet-sized cabin and Dan referred to it as being in "cockroach class." When one of us wanted to get dressed, the other had to huddle on the bottom bunk or step into the bathroom. But, not to worry. We had a ball!

After sailing past the fabulous Lady in the Harbor and giving her our special salute, we landed and stepped onto American soil once more. Now we're back in our house in Virginia and at this point have been in one place far longer than at any other time in our married life.

The kids? They're on their own and settled in careers that suit their individual personalities and talents and they give us reason to smile; we're very proud of them.

Satisfied that they are successfully launched, Dan and I are concentrating on us for a change. We're semi-retired these days and have time to travel for pleasure. Plus, we have the wonderful bonus of being grandparents now! That adds a delightful freshness to life at our age. And sometimes, when we enjoy sweet and quiet moments together in the evenings, we turn on the music, sit back and remember the adventure that lasted almost twenty-seven years.

All in all, it was a real trip for a couple who started out as kids in the small towns of Westminster, Maryland, and Caldwell, Idaho. It's rather odd to think that throughout those years we were American tax dollars at work. Thanks for the opportunity. We loved it!

CPSIA information can be obtained at www.ICGtesting.com
Printed in the USA
BVOW041116270513

321710BV00002B/225/P